It's Not Rocket Science

IT'S NOT
Rocket
Science

**7 Game-Changing Traits for
Uncommon Success**

MARY SPIO

A PERIGEE BOOK

PERIGEE
An imprint of Penguin Random House LLC
375 Hudson Street, New York, New York 10014

Perigee trade paperback ISBN: 978-0-399-16932-8

The Library of Congress has cataloged the Perigee hardcover edition as follows:

Spio, Mary.
It's not rocket science: 7 game-changing traits for uncommon success / Mary Spio.
pages cm
ISBN 978-0-399-16931-1 (hardback)
1. Success.   2. Self-actualization (Psychology).   I. Title.
BF637.585655   2015
650.1—dc23   2014038408

PUBLISHING HISTORY
Perigee hardcover edition / February 2015
Perigee trade paperback edition / February 2016

PRINTED IN THE UNITED STATES OF AMERICA

3   5   7   9   10   8   6   4   2

Text design by Kristin del Rosario

To my courageous parents,
whose curious spirit and compassionate care
filled me with a love for learning.
Your unwavering confidence compelled me to take
the dare to become more than I ever thought possible.
Your love afforded me the ability and the willingness
to respond to others' needs with the kind of dedication
that transcends all differences.

To my beloved sisters,
Grace, Tina, Regina and Joana,
as well as Meg Fynn and my precious
Mr. K., Prince Edward, Charles Biney and Joe Ofori.

INTRODUCTION

There is no passion to be found playing small—in settling for a life that is less than the one you are capable of living.

- NELSON MANDELA -

We are in a time in history like no other—an extraordinary moment when technology has given us amazing opportunities. What used to be the domain of only the privileged and connected is now accessible to all of us. Regardless of race, gender, education, age or circumstance, we all have access to the tools and resources needed to create the lifestyle that we desire. We live in a time when you can embrace your difference, do what you love and follow your passion. My own life is a testament to these times and just one example of the possibilities that abound for anyone with a dream and the willingness to work hard to achieve it.

By way of introduction, I am Mary A. Spio—deep space engineer, Internet entrepreneur, Game Changer. I will be your guide on this incredible journey beyond your wildest dreams. Imagine a life with no limits. That is our destination. Through examples, observations and hard-won insights, I will help you to crystallize your path, to pursue your dreams until they become reality, en-

couraging you to reach your full potential. How can I be so confi-
dent? I have traveled this path a few times with remarkable success.

Once a shoeless African child, I have had the opportunity to
sell technology to companies such as Boeing, to sit at the table
with leaders of some of the world's biggest companies and even to
change the movie industry. Who does that? Game Changers do
that! Game Changers are the ones who are bold enough and brash
enough to believe we can achieve our dreams and change the
world in the process.

As a U.S. speaker and unofficial ambassador of innovation, I
connect with thousands of people and see firsthand the pain and
frustration they are experiencing in a rapidly and ever-changing
world. I see it everywhere I go—from Job Corps seminars to the
most prestigious university symposiums and business conferences.
It is perhaps an underestimate that 50 percent of college graduates
will not find jobs, and the majority of people are doing jobs they
don't enjoy. These figures reflect not just an American phenomenon, but a global one. People see the world changing around them.
They are experiencing a sense of lack in a time of plenty and are
desperate to learn how to create the future they desire.

This book is a manifesto for reversing this situation, empowering readers to find their true passion and purpose—and challenging each one to make a big difference by changing something for
the better. In the past, you were told to get a good job and work
toward retirement. The new dream is achieving happiness in your
own way—creating a lifestyle of freedom by defining success your
way and doing meaningful, satisfying work. It's about purpose,
not position. It's about creating your own game rather than simply
accepting what someone else believes is possible for you.

This book is my offering to the Game Changer "tribe"—all of

us who not only dream of a better tomorrow, but who are committed to doing what it takes to create it. I wrote this book to be a catalyst for change. I hope to be that catalyst for you to pursue your dreams, to move to the next level and to find the best possible use for your talents and skills. I believe that when each of us pursues the highest and best use of our unique gifts, we can change our lives, change our communities and even change the world. My motto is: "When you share your light, you live in a brighter world." Through this book, I hope to help you find and light your spark so that you can make our world even brighter.

Being an entrepreneur is a pure exercise in self-mastery. It has tested and validated things I can now say I know to be true. This book is a collection of the discoveries, persuasions and resources that guided me in my journey. It is my playbook for a purposeful life. This is not a book about obtaining material wealth or about fearlessness and mindless rebellion. It is neither trendy nor sexy; just my truth and the guiding principles that have helped me find solace and more joy than I often feel deserving of.

The currency for change is not money, youth or education. The currency for great change is applied knowledge. Knowledge is not genetically encoded. Anyone and everyone can acquire the knowledge necessary to change their lives. Becoming a Game Changer and achieving uncommon success isn't rocket science. My aim is to share with you the knowledge and practical insights I've gained, as well as firsthand wisdom, guidance and experience from people who are living their life's passion while contributing in meaningful ways to their families, communities and the world at large.

To be a real Game Changer, you need both cheerleaders and coaches. No team ever won on cheers alone. This book attempts to be coach as well as cheerleader. It aims to tell you the things you may not want to hear and to be that voice telling you to "suck it up" and "give me ten more" when things get tough. It's also a play-book by a coach who is also an athlete—someone who has been in the game for a long time (and has the scars to prove it) and contin-ues to be in the game on a daily basis.

This book is your starting point. So get ready to journey to the unknown, take risks, break boundaries, speak out, set new stan-dards and achieve the meaningful success you've dreamed of. Get ready to change the game.

GAME CHANGERS

The people who are crazy enough to think that they can change the world are the ones who do.

- APPLE INC. -

I come from very humble beginnings. As a child, I ran around barefoot, looking like a poster child for Feed the Children, playing with my only toy—a stick. I didn't see my first computer until I was seventeen. Yet within a decade, I was working on a NASA Search for Extraterrestrial Intelligence (SETI) project and, shortly after, designing and launching satellites into space as a deep space scientist. By age twenty-nine, I was head of a satellite communications team that pioneered digital cinema technology that changed the motion picture industry. Since then, I've launched an award-winning magazine, despite the fact that I don't have a degree in journalism or any publishing industry experience. I've also founded two multimillion-dollar companies and worked with clients such as Microsoft Xbox and the Coca-Cola Company.

When people hear what I've been able to do, they assume I have some kind of special skills, maybe an extra twist on my DNA, massive frontal lobes in my brain or perhaps influential friends who pulled a few strings. That couldn't be further from the truth. What I have achieved is a testament to the opportunities and possibilities that abound for those who have a dream, are willing to work tirelessly and are crazy enough to believe they can change their corner of the world. So just how did I go from being a hungry child growing up in Ghana, West Africa, to deep space engineer, entrepreneur and Game Changer?

THE GAME CHANGER TRIBE

I've never had any true mentors, so I've had to rely on myself and learn from afar by watching others. When I came to the United States at age sixteen, I was completely on my own in a foreign country. In search of success, I started looking for successful people to model. I began by studying the actions of innovating pioneers like Bill Gates, Oprah Winfrey, George Lucas and many other dreamers who possessed the heroic courage to do what their heart desired. Before long, a pattern emerged—their successes were traceable to distinct actions and attributes. These became the ethos, the blueprint from which I would model my life. I followed this blueprint and everything changed. I too began to have success. Through my journey, I also noticed that while many people achieve success at some level, a few break through to achieve truly uncommon success. These are the people who are able to change our world in some way. They change the game, so to speak, by altering the way we think, the way we work or the way we live.

These Game Changers dare to paint outside the lines and have the courage to start new trends. They challenge old precepts and raise the standards. They choose to live life by their own rules rather than fit into a mold they are pushed into. They defy convention, disregard limits and ignore the odds to go beyond what most people perceive is possible. By allowing us to see our world in an entirely new light, they create greater value, understanding, joy and hope.

Some of the greatest figures throughout history were Game Changers. Nicolaus Copernicus was the first person to theorize that the sun, rather than the earth, is at the center of our universe. Four hundred years later, Albert Einstein's theory of relativity once again changed how humans understood our world. Alexander Fleming's discovery of penicillin led to the development of antibiotics and saved millions of lives. Gandhi secured India's independence from Great Britain through mass, nonviolent civil disobedience and inspired other leaders around the world, including Martin Luther King Jr. I could go on. Lewis and Clark, the Wright brothers, Henry Ford—the list of Game Changers is long. These people have become household names not simply because they achieved great personal success, but because they changed the game and moved the human race forward.

There are plenty of modern-day Game Changers as well: Bill Gates (Microsoft), Steve Jobs (Apple), Jeff Bezos (Amazon), Ted Turner (CNN), Oprah Winfrey (media), Sara Blakely (Spanx) and Michael DeBakey (heart surgeon pioneer), to name just a few. Game Changers come in all races, creeds, ages, genders and socioeconomic levels. You can find them in all walks of life, from the cerebral to the physical, from medicine to junk hauling. From the doctor who started a Facebook page that grew into the largest church on the planet (twenty-five million people and counting), to the Pakistani teenage girl who stood up to speak out against the Taliban's rules preventing girls from getting an education. From the sixty-four-year-old woman who became the first person to swim from Cuba to Florida, to the executive who went to work one day, got a pink slip, decided to start his own company and changed his life in the process. All of these people changed their respective "games" forever.

Of course, it's easy to identify Game Changers in hindsight. In retrospect, their achievements are obvious. But at the time, they often aren't recognized for their brilliance. They often must endure significant challenges, overcome obstacles and pass through the valley of the shadow of doubt again and again to reach the apex of unprecedented success.

CHANGING MY GAME

I was born in Syracuse, New York, to Ghanaian parents. A few years later, my parents returned to Ghana, West Africa. In 1981, the country was overtaken by military rogues and a new government came to power by coup d'état. Soldiers roamed the streets with guns, and there was a national curfew of 6:00 p.m. I knew children whose parents were taken away and put to death by firing squad. We endured days without food, and I can remember many nights crying myself to sleep from hunger.

There was one saving grace in the midst of the chaos and tragedy. We had a little black-and-white television set with one lone channel that came on at 6:00 p.m. and went off at midnight. There was no *American Idol, Dancing with the Stars* or Food Network. (It's still amazing to me that people watch other people cook, and that there are entire channels dedicated to fishing and golf.) Yet that little box was magic. It was our happy place, where we could escape reality and be entertained, informed and provoked into dialogue.

It feels like yesterday that I sat at my mother's feet watching a

TV show about space exploration. I remembering feeling the vibration of pure joy activated within me when I caught glimpses of vast unknown worlds. It started the fires of hope burning inside of me. My dreams were calling, and I developed a sense of urgency to find out more about the life I had seen inside of the little box.

As a teenager, I begged my parents to let me go back to America. They sold everything they could so that I could make this journey and find a better life. At age sixteen, I traveled alone from Ghana to America. Leaving my family and childhood behind was one of the most difficult things I've ever had to do.

I arrived at the Charlotte Douglas International Airport on September 29, 1989, at 9:39 p.m. I remember that day vividly. I felt like I had landed on the moon—this vast, unexplored place filled with lights, cars, skyscrapers. I knew exactly what the first man in space, Yuri Gagarin, meant when he uttered the words, "I see Earth. It's so beautiful!"

I lived with a host family in South Carolina while I completed high school. After graduation, my host family asked me to return to Ghana. But there was no way I was going back. I had other plans. While in Ghana, I had seen the movie *Coming to America* with Eddie Murphy, where young Prince Akeem goes to Queens, New York, in search of his bride. So the day after graduation, in the middle of the night, while everyone slept, I left for New York City in search of my own dreams and perhaps to bump into Prince Akeem. A bus and train ride later, I arrived at Grand Central Station. I played "eeny, meeny, miney, moe" and landed on the number three train—last stop New Lots, Brooklyn.

New Lots became my home, where I joyfully lived in the heart of the ghetto surrounded by gang members, pimps and preachers. With that audacious move, I instantly became the ultimate latchkey kid—living on my own in New York while my parents were thousands of miles away. You realize what it means to be on your own the first time you have to use your own money to buy trivial things like toothpaste and toilet paper. I was 100 percent responsible for my well-being. Survival sparked my inner flame to succeed, and the engines began to rev.

Not knowing where to start, I got a job at McDonald's to pay the rent. I knew I could flip burgers and mop floors. I endured the harsh prejudices that some people can pile upon those whose true selves are yet to be unmasked. Each day, I yearned for respect and dignity, not only for myself, but also for those who thought like me, looked like me and lived like me. The steel was being forged. My emotional hunger fed by the cold reality of my painful existence tossed and turned the dreamer inside of me. I knew then that the sleeper must awaken.

Late one night while watching TV, I saw a commercial about doing more by 5:00 a.m. than most people do in a day. I thought, "Whatever it is, sign me up!" The next day, I went down to join the army. But fate intervened. In the hallway, I saw a mountain of a man with a big smile and even bigger biceps—the air force recruiter. With visions of me marching amid thousands of airmen just like him flooding my mind, he easily convinced me to join the air force. (At that age, your reasons for making life-changing decisions are not always rational. "Why did you join the air force?" "The recruiter was cute, duh!" I was a seventeen-year-old girl after all.)

It was in the air force that I learned the inner workings of media and technology. I became a satellite communications and wideband technician. I was in Turkey during Desert Storm as part of the advent team that set up communications for the troops so they could communicate with one another and with base. One day, after I managed to repair a circuit board and some terminals, an engineer told me I should consider going back to school to study engineering. I applied for the Scholarship for Outstanding Airmen and was the only person selected from all of the U.S. Forces in Europe that year. I was starting to hear words like *brilliant*, *outstanding* and *awesome* associated with my name, and I liked it. I liked it a lot!

After the air force, I attended Syracuse University where I majored in engineering with a focus in deep space science and a minor in psychology. I've always been a child of two worlds. I love things and I love people, and I'm always seeking opportunities to connect both worlds. In fact, I put myself through college making connections as a matchmaker.

I continued on to Georgia Tech for graduate studies in deep space communications. After grad school, the world opened up to me. I designed and sent satellites into space, including orbital design for the Iridium 77 satellite constellation. As a satellite applications engineer at PanAmSat, my expertise was designing television networks. I worked with every major network from HBO to Disney and designed the entire network for Japanese Fuji TV from a blank piece of paper. Then Boeing came calling. I was hand-selected to join two other people in creating Boeing Digital Cinema, where we engineered the technology to digitally deliver movies all over the globe. (*Star Wars: Episode II* was one of the first movies digitally delivered globally.) I was the sole inventor for several digital cinema technology patents.

Today, I am the president and CEO of Next Galaxy Corp.—a

leading consumer virtual reality technology and digital media
company. I also founded Gen2Media, now Vidaroo, an emerging
video technology and production company. Through my companies, I've had the opportunity to work with some of the largest
media companies and entertainment personalities in the world
(think Xbox and the Black Eyed Peas). Recently I was selected by
the U.S. Department of State as a speaker and innovation evange-
list. I've spoken in or visited China, Mexico, Pakistan, Russia and
South Africa, spreading the goodwill of the American Dream, innovation and entrepreneurship. Not bad at all for a former "poster
child" for world hunger.

I don't tell you my story to flaunt my accomplishments. My
story is my victory dance, my song of eternal gratitude to the spirit
of defiance, compassion, focus and the power of the dreamer's
spirit. And that is why I share it with you—it is my whisper of
hope to the other dreamers out there who desperately yearn for
more. I tell you my story to prove to you that if I can do it, you
can too—no matter where you are in your life. I hope that mo-
mentarily viewing the world through my eyes will stoke the fire
within you to pursue your own dreams, and achieve them.

I have become courageous—although not fearless—in the
course of my journey, and my goal with this book is to get you
there too. If I can alter the course of my life, anyone can. My
vision is to build a tribe of dreamers and Game Changers who will
impact our world in a big way. I believe there is greatness in each
of us. My mission is to wake that sleeper within you and help you
find and create your path to a future that is beyond belief.

YOU ARE A CHANGER

If you have a vision, a passion or a dream within your heart, you are no different from Albert Einstein, Gandhi, Martin Luther King Jr., Oprah Winfrey, Bill Gates, Mark Zuckerberg or anyone else who has ever changed the game and achieved uncommon success. You may not have a vision to change the world, but neither did they in the beginning. They simply had a vision to change their little corner of the world. We all hold different keys for moving our world forward, and the beautiful thing is we do not know who holds which keys. Each and every one of us is a Game Changer in the making; we just may not realize it yet.

What piece of the world or part of your circumstances do you want to change? The "game" is different for each person. Perhaps you want to be the first in your family to go to college. Or maybe you want to lose weight or

> The game is whatever you want it to be, and you are the one who can change it.

live a healthier lifestyle. Do you want to break familial patterns of alcoholism or addiction or improve the relationships in your life? Do you have a big idea that could change the way business operates, or an initiative that will make a positive difference in your community? Maybe you just want to live life on your own terms. The game is whatever you want it to be, and you are the one who can change it. In fact, you may be the only one who can change it, and that is why the world needs you to step up and become a Game Changer.

My father used to tell me, "Small hinges swing big doors." The smallest act, the smallest change, can start a chain reaction that eventually impacts the world. Almost every Game Changer started with the tiniest seed of an idea that grew into something big. I didn't set out to change anything except my circumstances. But in changing my circumstances, I eventually changed the movie distribution industry. You are one hinge that has the power to open big doors. You can break through to uncommon success and a limitless life. You are a Game Changer.

PART ONE

7 Key Traits That Fuel Game Changers' Success

Many people think Game Changers have some kind of advantage, luck, extraordinary talent or privilege that separates them from the rest. There is, in fact, something that separates them from the rest, but it's not any of these things. As I've studied the highest achievers over the last twenty years, I've searched for the Game Changers' formula for success. As a scientist, I am intrigued by the lawfulness of the universe. Every phenomenon has a traceable formula for its existence and its duplication. My aim has been to come close to a formula for this uncommon achievement that could be duplicated by anyone, anywhere. Uncommon success is not reserved for the rich or the famous or the intellectuals. Uncommon success can be achieved by each of us.

I believe the secret to becoming a Game Changer is a two-part formula. First, Game Changers possess certain characteristics that are the foundation of their success. The second part of the formula for game-changing success is to discover your greatness and live a life of design by working in the center of your passion, potential and purpose. In Part One, you will discover the seven key traits for achieving uncommon success:

- Unbridled Creativity
- Radical Passion

- Active Compassion
- Obsessive Focus
- Relentless Hustle
- Extreme Audacity
- Pit Bull Tenacity

Although we are not necessarily born with all of these traits, each of us has the ability to cultivate them. The real capital for greatness is not money, but developing these traits. In the following chapters, we will take a closer look at each trait. You will meet inspiring Game Changers who exemplify that trait and learn practical tips for how you can enhance that trait within yourself. Cultivate these Game Changer traits by design, and soon they will become your default.

Unbridled Creativity

Creating a new theory is not like destroying an old barn and
erecting a skyscraper in its place. It is rather like climbing a
mountain, gaining new and wider views, discovering unexpected connections between our starting points and its rich
environment.

- ALBERT EINSTEIN -

If you've ever asked, "Why . . . ?" If you've ever wondered,
"How . . . ?" If you've ever thought, "I can do it differently!" Then
you have the prerequisite to become a Game Changer. Game
Changers are creative innovators. They imagine the possibilities
and then take action to transform ideas into reality.

There's a lot of talk today about creativity, about what it is and
how to have more of it. Creativity comes from untethered imagination and curiosity. You start with a blank slate and imagine all
the possibilities. Then you nurture those possibilities with curiosity and cultivate them with creativity until they become tangible.
The result is innovation—new ideas and concepts of profound
impact that literally change the game as we know it. We go up into
the high country of the mind and breathe the thinner air to be
truly creative.

Creativity doesn't happen by accident. It is the result of high
imagination, deep curiosity and intelligent direction. The goal of
this chapter is to inspire the creative innovator in you, to fuel the

mind-building revolution needed to develop the answers and solutions that our world desperately needs and eagerly awaits.

IMAGINATION IS THE BIRTHPLACE OF GAME-CHANGING IDEAS

Not having much as a child, I was forced to rely on my imagination. I enjoyed vivid flights of fancy—seeing, feeling, tasting, hearing, touching and experiencing every detail in my mind. I remember feeling the breeze and tasting the salty air as I read *The Old Man and the Sea*. Long before I ever set foot in America, I dreamed of the streets of America's great cities. On hot days in Ghana, I'd "visit" New York City in the winter, making snow angels in the fluffy snow in Central Park.

When I finally arrived in the United States and saw all the great American icons that the world has come to know, I had a moment of insight: Everything we see in existence today started as simple thoughts and dreams in someone's mind. Imagination is the starting point of everything humankind has created, and it is what moves the world forward. Truly, life is what we imagine it to be!

Imagination is the place where ideas are born, the seeds of vision are planted, problems are solved and change begins. Imagination creates a future not based on what is known, but what is possible. Many of my best inventions have come during my visualizations and flights of fancy. If you doubt the power of imagination, consider creative visionary Arthur C. Clarke.

Most people know Clarke as a science fiction writer and author of one of the most influential novels and movies of our time, *2001: A Space Odyssey*. But Clarke also wrote scientific publications on space, energy and the oceans. In 1945, he wrote a scientific article about his vision of putting telecommunications satellites in geosynchronous orbit miles above the earth. Decades later, engineers made his vision a reality. (He once said in an interview that he didn't patent what, at the time, was an incredibly radical idea because he didn't think it would see the light of day in his lifetime.) The geosynchronous orbit is known as the Clarke Orbit in his honor, and the collection of satellites in these orbits is known as the Clarke Belt.

Thanks to Clarke and his imagination, you can watch six hundred television channels through your satellite dish, your smartphone can direct you to the closest gas station and you can physically see just about any location on the planet with Google Earth. Clarke also imagined and predicted space shuttles, supercomputers, lightning-quick communications and that man would reach the moon. Science fiction became science fact . . . all because of one man's imagination.

Science was Clarke's passion. Just like Clarke, your imagination can be a door to your passion. When your mind wanders, where it goes and what you imagine is a clue to your dreams and desires. The things you see are the true essence of what you want. Your imagination preplays what is possible. And in today's world, if you can imagine it, chances are you can make it happen.

> In today's world,
> if you can imagine it,
> chances are you can
> make it happen.

Technology has made available the tools and resources to turn dreams into reality for just about everyone. Anyone who has the courage to ask "What if . . ." can define a new vision for our time or change the way we live our lives.

Imagination is a wide-open space where the possibilities are truly endless. With imagination, every single person has the ability to create their desired future, to express thoughts and ideas and to design a vision of the unknown. The beauty of imagination is that it is free, unrestricted and available to each and every one of us. Unlike IQ, which is fixed, imagination is infinite, limitless.

Dr. Patricia Bath is a Game Changer in the field of ophthalmology. "I am in my most natural state when I am simply imagining, thinking, dreaming. Being a dreamer frees the mind to have 'time out' to be creative," she said. Albert Einstein was also a dreamer who often took flights of imagination while in school, pondering things such as traveling at the speed of light, why the sky was blue and other topics that weren't taught in school. Einstein once said, "Knowledge is limited to all we now know and understand, while imagination embraces the entire world, and all there ever will be to know and understand." That quote reminds me of a story my father tells of a little boy named Kwame.

One day in Kwame's kindergarten class, the teacher asked the students to draw a picture of anything they wanted. Long after all the other children had completed their drawings, Kwame was still busily drawing away. Finally, his teacher asked him what he was drawing. Deep in concentration, Kwame answered, "A picture of God."

His teacher laughed, "But, Kwame, no one knows what God looks like."

Kwame looked up, his eyes as wide as plates, beaming with excitement. "Then they'll know when I'm done with my picture!"

Now, there is a Game Changer in the making! Imagination is the blank sheet of paper on which Game Changers paint a picture of what is possible. You are a Game Changer. What picture will you paint for the world?

CURIOSITY DRIVES ACTION

Imagination is the fuel that drives curiosity—the quest for knowledge, the search for answers to the questions our imagination poses. Many people think of curiosity as an intellectual endeavor. Game Changers understand that curiosity involves action. Game Changers are not merely dreamers, they are also doers.

I've always been curious about "the possibilities," and I was fortunate to have parents who encouraged this curiosity from a very early age. I remember as though it were yesterday, sitting at my mother's feet watching that program on space exploration. I was filled with so much excitement, and from that point on, I wanted to learn as much as I could about space. I read books. I dreamed of the stars and what it all meant.

Throughout my life I have followed my curiosity, and it has served me well. As a child, I was fascinated with how information is transmitted from one point to another. How did someone far away get their voice or music to come out over the radio in my house? This curiosity led me to take apart our radios and, many years later, study engineering. While studying engineering, I became curious about how satellites stay in space and transmit information to earth. That led me to learn about deep space science, orbital mechanics and satellite communications. The more I indulged my curiosity, the more answers I gained. The more answers I gained, the more opportunities I created, which in turn led me to develop some game-changing technologies.

Curiosity opens the aperture of life to allow more knowledge and understanding to enter. The curious mind is always learning, always looking for opportunities to acquire knowledge and a greater understanding of the world around us. From knowledge comes great insight. When you follow your curiosity, you acquire information, perspective and life experiences that lead to "light-bulb moments." All of this "data" is filed in your mental database for retrieval in the future. You never know when some mathematical equation, a strange custom from a different culture or a random piece of information that doesn't seem like it would be useful will turn out to be the very thing you need to know in order to solve a problem or develop a new idea.

As a little girl, I was curious about what lay beyond the world I knew. One of my favorite books was about a shepherd boy from Peru named Pedro and his life in the mountains near the Inca ruins of Machu Picchu. Decades later, I met a gentleman at an event, and he mentioned he was from Peru. I immediately perked up with interest and began talking about Machu Picchu. When he asked if I had visited, I just smiled and explained that I'd read about it in a book. We ultimately formed a friendship that led to my working with the Peru Tourism Association, and it all stemmed from a conversation based on a book I read when I was ten years old.

The key to creativity is having viable options, and this is why curiosity is a prerequisite for creativity. Options are a function of the breadth and depth of your knowledge and experience. If you don't exercise your curiosity, chances are you'll miss a lot of potential opportunities. Every piece of information, every life experience, is like a tool in your creativity toolbox. When a situation arises down the road, you have the tools to pull out and use. The more tools in your toolbox (that is, the more knowledge and experience you have), the more creative you will be.

Apple founder Steve Jobs once said, "Much of what I stumbled into by following my curiosity and intuition turned out to be priceless later on." For example, while at Reed College, Steve noticed calligraphy posters everywhere. Intrigued by the beautiful fonts, he decided to take a calligraphy class. He described it as "beautiful, historical, artistically subtle in a way that science can't capture, and I found it fascinating." It was in this class that he learned about serif and san serif typefaces, as well as the nuances and subtleties of typography. A decade later, while designing the first Macintosh computer, he drew inspiration from what he had learned in that calligraphy class, and the Mac became the first computer with beautiful typography. If Steve Jobs had not followed his curiosity and taken that course in college, the future of personal computers would have been very different. His curiosity started a creative revolution.

Dr. Harry Lewis has got to be one of the most important professors in higher education today. Call it luck, call it fate, call it what you will, but not many college professors can say they had two of the world's biggest innovators in their classroom. Microsoft founder Bill Gates and Facebook founder Mark Zuckerberg were both students of Dr. Lewis. (Dr. Lewis is also the author of several books, including *Excellence Without a Soul* and *Blown to Bits: Your Life, Liberty and the Pursuit of Happiness After the Digital Explosion*.)

I had the opportunity to interview Dr. Lewis and asked him what traits these two Game Changers shared. He talked about their curiosity—not just curiosity in computer science, but their desire to see how the world at large works. He also talked about their love for learning and the breadth and depth of experiences they exposed themselves to. "[Gates and Zuckerberg] were multi-dimensional," he observed. "They were not narrowly technically interested. They were interested in lots of different fields. They had a deep interest in learning things that were outside of the classroom and understanding how topics they were learning about in one area might make a difference in another."

This multidimensional curiosity is what allowed Gates and Zuckerberg to see our world creatively and connect the dots in ways that were profound. And it's the same curiosity that Steve Jobs possessed. Do you see a pattern here? Game Changers are multidimensional thinkers. They have a deep curiosity that reaches across many disciplines and topics.

Nobody changes the game by error. Even "accidental" discoveries and innovations are rooted in imagination and curiosity. As a child, Mike Gallagher was always curious about networks and how they worked. He also had a neighbor who worked for the phone company, and Mike would climb in the back of his truck and scrutinize all the phone equipment. It was no surprise, then, that decades later Mike and his company completely changed the telecommunications industry by bringing broadband to the masses.

> Game Changers are multidimensional thinkers.

To be a Game Changer, you must commit to becoming a life-long learner. Although all humans are innately curious, many of us have lost our inquisitive nature. Irrespective of culture, all babies attentively explore their surroundings. But over time, many people get sidetracked by the responsibilities of everyday living and lose their sense of wonder.

It is time to rekindle the fire of curiosity within you. You are naturally curious about things you're good at. Follow that voice. It's usually very faint; perhaps that is the reason many of us ignore it. Your purpose whispers—it never screams—and through curiosity and learning you can discover it. Follow your passions and saturate yourself with as many life experiences as possible, because everything you go through better prepares you for the future. Even difficult and painful life experiences trigger curiosity and fascination. The wounded often become the best at healing because they passionately search for ways to heal their hurts and relieve their pain. In life, your assets and liabilities are often one and the same. It's all a matter of perspective.

Let your imagination run free and then let your curiosity drive the search for answers, meaning and purpose.

FEED YOUR CURIOSITY

Open the aperture of your life by broadening your experiences. Here is my short list of ways to feed your curiosity:

- READ. Bill Gates is reportedly a voracious reader who at a very early age read the entire *World Book Encyclopedia* series. His parents encouraged his curiosity by buying him any book he wanted. My father always brought a book home to me each time he traveled, and now I do the same for my son. Today, I feed my mind with history books, classic novels and even books from various religions. I especially love biographies because they provide concentrated information about successful, fascinating people, and I can learn from their victories and mistakes.

- LEARN AS MUCH AS YOU CAN ABOUT DIFFERENT SUB-
  JECTS. Study history. Take a class or attend a lecture about
  a subject you're interested in. Research Nobel Prize win-
  ners and their work. Do a science project or build an electronic kit.

- MAKE IT A GOAL TO NOTICE OR LEARN SOMETHING
  NEW EVERY DAY. Watch a foreign movie. Participate in a
  new game, sport or form of exercise. Visit an art or historical
  museum. Study a foreign language or learn how to play an
  instrument. Spend an afternoon investigating more about
  the world's problems and challenges.

CREATIVITY CONNECTS THE DOTS

One of the biggest misconceptions about creativity is that you're
either born with it or you're not. I believe creativity is less a matter
of nature and more a matter of nurture. In other words, creativity
is not as much about how you're born as your approach. It is a
process, a mind-set, a learned way of being, and any learned be-
havior can be acquired and enhanced.

As the cofounder and managing partner of an award-winning
marketing and advertising agency, Sherman Wright knows a thing
or two about creativity. "I think everybody has creative thoughts,"
he told me during an interview. "The human mind is creative
within itself. The question is, are you willing to put yourself out
there—to go against the grain or to do things that may not be accepted by the masses—to bring ideas to life? Yes, I think everybody is creative, but I don't think everyone knows how to act on
creativity."

Creativity is about "connecting the dots"—making connections between things that have never before been linked. It is the ability to recognize the possibilities that exist within any scenario and the opportunities in every situation. Changing the game starts with seeing the unseen within even the ordinary. Out of a plain slab of marble, Michelangelo carved his best work. German philosopher Arthur Schopenhauer once said, "Talent hits a target no one else can hit. Genius hits a target no one else can see." Creative solutions and breakthroughs come from viewing something differently and discovering what others have missed. Patents for novel ideas, processes and methodologies are simply the tangible results of someone seeing something differently than the world had ever seen it before. Paradigms shift when people come along who see how to connect the dots, apply multiple perspectives and build a bridge between unrelated ideas.

Sherman Wright defines creativity this way: "Creativity is the ability to see things differently, the ability to solve problems in unique and different ways, the ability to inspire and engage others to do things in new and different ways. So for me, creativity is transformation and evolution."

Imagination and curiosity are the prerequisites for creativity. Creativity stems from the willingness to let your imagination run wild, to be curious, to experiment and to dare to be different. The more possibilities you imagine and the more knowledge and experience you gain through following your curiosity, the larger your information database and the greater your chances of connecting never-before-connected dots. The more you use your imagination and curiosity muscles, the more creative you'll become.

While working as a satellite applications engineer designing television networks, I always wondered why satellite delivery wasn't used for movie delivery, as both seemed like similar concepts to me. But I figured someone must have already had that idea. Little ol' me couldn't possibly have come up with an idea that no one else had thought of before. A few years later, I was offered an opportunity to work with Lucasfilm to investigate a solution for the movie studios to deliver movies. I came up with a novel process and technique for delivering movies via satellite. I am listed as the sole inventor on the patent, which is owned by Boeing. The technology, used worldwide today to distribute movies digitally, is a tremendous cost savings and an efficient way to track ticketing.

While working on the digital movie delivery, I also became curious about the possibility of having alternate endings to movies. I developed other technologies such as real-time streaming and making alternate endings a reality. With my new knowledge of the film industry, I came up with a web-based technology for online streaming of video content. It was first used by entertainment retailers such as Suncoast Motion Picture Company and later by media companies such as Tribune News and Clear Channel.

The information and experiences I gathered along the way formed the dots that enabled me to develop these technologies. I pulled elements out of my information and experience database and connected them to create something new. These technologies have changed their respective industries, but started as "what ifs" in my head. In my conversation with Dr. Harry Lewis about his star students Bill Gates and Mark Zuckerberg, he said, "Very often the people who are the real Game Changers in society are the people who figure out how to put different things together. There are lots of opportunities for people who let their creativity rule and come up with new ideas. Ideas come from putting together these different fields of knowledge. Zuckerberg's genius was not in computer science or in sociology or psychology, but he was taking courses in all those areas. His genius was in figuring out that you could take the social networking that sociologists were talking about and actually do it online."

Alberto Ruiz is another inspiring Game Changer. He has created a genre of art that is original to him, drawing illustrations of the female form that are utterly unique. "Creativity is the sensitivity to perceive what is not apparent to others. It is also the intuitiveness to recognize the sublime in the mundane, the grotesque in the majestic. A regular person sees a red apple—no less, no more, depending on his or her state of being or the time of day. A creative person sees yellows, greens, purples, blues, sin, desire, hunger, god, youth, decay, death and an infinite amount of possibilities. We all can be creative in any field or profession. I've even heard the term 'creative accountant' a few times."

When I asked Alberto about his definition of art, he shared, "I'm not concerned with what is taught or what is shown. If an object or a performance elicits an emotional response from my brain, whether Rembrandt or Simon Bisley, that is art. Traditionalist thinking equates to narrow-mindedness; van Gogh and his art were regarded as garbage by the traditionalists of his time." It sounds like van Gogh was a Game Changer too.

Alberto's sentiments echo those I heard from Dr. Lewis about Gates and Zuckerberg: "I taught these two incredibly innovative people, but when I knew them they were just somewhat impatient, irreverent people. They were very smart, but they were not necessarily staying between the lines at every moment. They were being creative in ways that the faculty didn't necessarily recognize or appreciate at that time."

Game Changers are creative people who are audacious—willing to take risks or push the boundaries of what's possible. They are spontaneous, truly kids at heart. (Play is a great way to exercise your creative muscle.) Creative minds are unafraid of what others think, and they see failure as feedback. In response to comments that his experiments to develop a practical lightbulb had failed, Thomas Edison is reported to have said, "I have not failed. I've just found ten thousand ways that won't work." The creative process is about learning as much as possible from the journey and finding the best possible outcome.

While many associate creativity with the arts, creativity comes in all forms. Creativity is pushing the boundaries in whatever area your passion lies. It can be seen in all facets of life, from academics to entertainment and everything in between. Today, we see the convergence of science and art everywhere. The artist must think like the scientist, and the scientist like the artist. We are at a point in time when form and function are equally important. Most people think that Apple is one of the most technologically innovative companies, but this is actually not true. Their magic is twofold. First is their uncanny ability to marry science and art. The second is that they are masters of reinvention. Apple did not invent the personal computer, MP3 player, smartphone or tablet. Instead, they looked at these existing products and had the innovative insight to make them better. Apple is by far the most innovative company in making computers, music players, smartphones and tablets both practical and intuitive—that is the essence of creativity.

If you haven't yet heard of graphene, you will soon enough. Andre Geim and Kostya Novoselov won the 2010 Nobel Prize in physics for their work to develop this one-atom-thick sheet of graphite (yes, the same graphite that is used in pencils) with truly incredible properties. Graphene is flexible, harder than a diamond, stronger than steel and a better conductor of electricity and heat than any material discovered so far. The potential uses for graphene are almost infinite. One day, your contact lenses could be your alarm clock. A necktie might be able to warn you of an impending heart attack based on changes in your vital signs and automatically call your doctor or an ambulance. Graphene fabric could make military uniforms the ultimate camouflage by changing colors to match their background, much like a chameleon. Graphene is a massive opportunity just waiting for creative people all over the planet to connect the dots.

Often people say to me, "I have this idea but it's kind of silly." No idea is silly. Ten years ago, the idea of making conductive fabric out of layered one-atom-thick graphite seemed ridiculous. Now it's just years away from becoming reality. Many of the greatest innovations we have today started as tiny seeds in someone's head that grew into giant solutions.

You have within you the seed of the next game-changing innovation. Opportunities are everywhere. You are limited only by your imagination. No one who has ever lived in the history of mankind has your imagination or has had your life experiences. You alone possess your unique combination of knowledge and perspective. And that makes you extraordinarily qualified to see a connection that no one else has ever seen. You possess the perfect recipe for creating something no one else has ever created. You are a Game Changer.

———————

I always tell people that, fundamentally, success is about what I call my five Ps: Prayer, Purpose, Passion, Persistence and Patience. I don't care what you're doing in life; those five things come into play. Being a man who believes in God, faith has been my most powerful asset. Purpose is about asking why you're doing something and how you can benefit others. When you think about passion, it's that fire in your belly, that which you have been put on this earth to do. That follows on your purpose. Persistence . . . There are going to be bad days. There are going to be times when things don't go right. You've got to push through. Patience—it's going to take longer than you expected. It's not going to happen when you want it to happen, but it will happen. I think if you can be comfortable within that portfolio of characteristics, success is inevitable.

—SHERMAN WRIGHT,
COFOUNDER, COMMONGROUND

Radical Passion

———

I would rather die of passion than of boredom.

- VINCENT VAN GOGH -

A crucial aspect of the Game Changer movement is redefining success as living with passion and purpose. As humans, we all have an inexplicable need to express our gifts and live our purpose. When we choose to live in the center of our passions, brilliance emerges, and we find our greatness—that area that allows us to offer ourselves to the world for our highest and best use.

In the past, rather than following their passions and purpose, people fought for jobs. We were taught to pick a "safe" career whether it fascinated us or not. We were conditioned to think that we couldn't make a living doing what we loved. So we tucked our dreams away or pursued them as a hobby. Then we watched the clock . . . and counted the years . . . and waited until retirement to enjoy life.

But happiness is not to be put on layaway and retrieved at retirement. It should be a part of our everyday existence.

Fortunately, times are changing. Today, the battle is to design a lifestyle around one's passions. People want to enjoy the work they do by turning their passions into meaningful businesses and careers, and technology has made that dream possible for virtually anyone, anywhere. Instead of working to survive or get by, now it's possible to work for joy (and money). Instead of working toward retirement, people pursue their passions as long as possible because they *want* to rather than *have* to.

Game-changing advertising guru Sherman Wright understands firsthand the distinction between a passion-based career and a passionless job. "Coming out of high school, we were told to go where the money was. I grew up in Houston, Texas, with NASA right down the street, and a couple of my friends' fathers were aerospace engineers there. So I chose aerospace engineering as a major in college. It wasn't based on interest, but what I thought made sense at the time.

"I realized after just one week in an engineering class at Texas A&M that I had no clue what was going on. I changed my major to journalism—again, not based on interest, but on what degree I could get in a timely fashion. Later, I took an advertising course, and a blurb in a textbook about advertising legend Tom Burrell really piqued my interest. Shortly after that, I was on a date and saw the movie *Boomerang*. When I saw Eddie Murphy's character, advertising exec Marcus Graham, I thought he had the coolest job in the world. I thought, 'That's what I want to do!' My passion for advertising started from a blurb in a business book at an engineering school and a movie!"

In many respects, the fight to live one's passion—to create a lifestyle intertwined with passion—is the very essence of entrepreneurship. Many successful businesses are tangible portraits of their founders' passions. Hughes Aircraft Company was born from Howard Hughes's love of aviation. Virgin Group came out of Richard Branson's passion for music. Starbucks grew from one store to a global phenomenon because of Howard Schultz's passion for an exceptional cup of coffee shared with friends in a welcoming coffeehouse environment.

Creating a passion-driven lifestyle is an intentional choice. When I graduated from college, I very intentionally selected a job based on work that revolved around my passions. I wanted the work itself to be the reward. I knew if I did that, success would follow. I had read about a company called PanAmSat and its founder, Rene Anselmo. I loved his story, his vision and the exciting opportunities his company could provide. I passed on several job offers that involved more money because I wanted to be somewhere where I could apply my passion. It might sound cliché, but it's true: When you love what you do, you don't work a day in your life. If you align your passion with your work, work and play become one. Work becomes your life reward rather than something you must survive.

> If you align your passion with your work, work and play become one.

PASSION IS THE SPARK THAT STARTS THE FIRE OF CHANGE

Every fire starts with a spark. Passion is the spark that ignites game-changing creativity, audacity, compassion, tenacity, focus and drive. It is the rocket fuel that launches dreams, a powerful force that guides Game Changers' thoughts, actions and ultimately their lives.

In relentlessly following their passions, Game Changers set

new standards by shattering our preconceived notions of what is possible. Michael Jordan's passion for basketball and to be a champion forever changed the sport. After a sophomore classmate beat him out for the final spot on his high school varsity basketball team, Jordan used what felt like a crushing defeat to fuel his obsessive passion for the game. And it served him well, as he raised the bar for elite players in the NBA. During his career, he led the Chicago Bulls to six national championships, earned the NBA's Most Valuable Player award five times and led the U.S. Olympic team to gold medals in 1984 and 1992.

Engineering major turned advertising executive Sherman Wright is at the forefront of the multicultural marketing revolution. He defied the odds and achieved staggering success as the founder of the highly respected, award-winning agency Common-Ground, with clients such as the Illinois Lottery, Coca-Cola, Coors, Bacardi, Nike and Nissan. Sherman has changed the advertising and marketing game as we know it by completely altering the way marketers approach diversity. Recognizing that African American and Hispanic populations are setting cultural trends that will play a tremendous, game-changing role in the growth and success of American brands, Sherman embraces a philosophy that focuses on the connections we all share while leveraging and celebrating our differences.

I asked Sherman how he defines a Game Changer. "I think Game Changers are people who understand how to evolve the system," he said. "I went into advertising and created the way I and my agency do things with a cross-consumer philosophy. What we find is that clients and other agencies are adapting their approaches and philosophies based on our success and results. Perhaps we have helped evolve advertising to the next level."

While Game Changers like Michael Jordan and Sherman Wright raise the bar to unprecedented levels in existing "games," other Game Changers create entirely new industries, genres or categories just to house their passion. They are able to hit a target previously unseen. Once that target has been hit, they open the aperture of understanding wider for all of us. Marc and Shanon Parker are just such Game Changers. They are the brains and the brawn behind Parker Brothers Concepts. Marc and Shanon create one-of-a-kind, functional vehicles from the most amazing machines seen in movies, comic books, TV shows and their customers' imaginations. Shanon is the chief designer and a fabricator; Marc is the engineering and fabrication specialist. Their motto is: "If you can dream it, we can build it."

I had the opportunity to interview these incredible game-changing brothers on the set of their popular television show *Dream Machines.* "We grew up really poor, and I always wanted a Green Machine (like a Big Wheel)," Marc shared. "When we got older, we decided we wanted to build something crazy from our youth. We built toys on the side as a hobby, so we said, 'Let's build a giant Green Machine.' That's where it started."

But that was only the beginning. The Parker brothers decided to leave their construction jobs behind and create a business around their passion. "We have always been into cars and motorcycles, but the things we liked weren't available in the marketplace. So we decided to start creating them on our own," Marc said. "A few things that we built ended up on the Internet. People started calling, wanting us to build this and that, and the business evolved from there."

One of the first Parker Brothers' vehicles that got a lot of attention was a neutron bike inspired by the movie *Tron*. "It was one of those bikes that everybody said was completely unbuildable," said Shanon. "For us, the challenge is to find a way to build something that most people think can't be built. We won't do something if it has already been done."

When I asked if they see themselves as Game Changers, Marc said: "I think we are Game Changers. I really do. That's what our whole philosophy has always been. From the beginning, we wanted to be innovators, not imitators. We want to do it completely different, and that tends to change the game. We look at the stuff we did a couple of years ago and some of the stuff coming out in the market now, and we can see our influence in the new products."

Shanon agreed. "I don't think we started out intending to change the game. But I do see people starting to follow suit, saying, 'Hey, you're right, there is another way of doing this.' People are following the trend we started."

Marc and Shanon have an intense passion to push the envelope of engineering in the motor vehicle industry. "What's going to be available fifty years from now—that's where we want to be," said Marc. "It gives us our own little niche in the market that nobody else really messes with."

GAME CHANGERS LIVE IN THE CENTER OF THEIR PASSIONS

Game Changers live in the center of their passions. They make their passion their life's focus and obsession. Laurie Clark is a Game Changer in the truest sense of the word. She has changed the game many times, in many ways. First, she changed the course of her family's history by being the first person in her family to attend college. But that was just the beginning of her "firsts." She was the youngest divisional manager at Staples and the youngest and one of the first female senior executives at Staples.

When I asked Laurie about the role passion has played in her success, she shared, "When you have a drive to do something that you love, you think about it all the time. You think about it when you get up in the morning, and you think about it at night. Your true passion is part of your everyday living. It is not an encapsulated drive to succeed or an idea that you get and you develop. Passion is every day of my life . . . and it comes to me—that's passion."

> There isn't just one way to live a passion-driven lifestyle.

Laurie continued, "I'll be driving down the street and see something and it sparks an idea. I'll be watching TV, and it sparks an idea. I'll be reading a newspaper, and it's on my mind. I have an inspiration, and I stop and I write it down or call someone. My passion is lived every day of my life."

As I've studied Game Changers to learn the formula behind their greatness, I discovered that while all live in the center of their passions, they express those passions very differently. There isn't just one way to live a passion-driven lifestyle. Some pursue multiple passions while others pursue a singular passion in a multitude of ways.

Game Changers who chase a single passion exponentially have the ability to recognize their passion everywhere, in every situation. In yoga, the word "Namaste" is an acknowledgment of the soul in one person by the soul in another, meaning we recognize in others what is also within ourselves. Many Game Changers have what I call Namaste moments, when they recognize their passion in a situation, place or thing. It has the feel of a baby kicking within them or a distant voice whispering in their ear.

In living his passion, Noah Graj has had many Namaste moments. Noah is a brand strategist at Graj + Gustavsen. He is also a serial entrepreneur with a host of passion-driven enterprises. "One of my biggest passions revolves around the concept of growth," Noah told me recently. "For me, it has always been about the process of planting a seed and helping it grow and bear fruit. I love that process very much. I always incorporate that idea into my life, and I incorporated it into the different companies I created—Urban Farmers, Dream Talks and a couple other things I play around with."

Noah began his passion-centered lifestyle when he started Urban Farmers fifteen years ago. He shares the story of its germination on his website (urbanfarmers.org):

I had a small place [in New York City] that was overwhelmed by plant life. So much so that it spilled over to my fire escape. . . . I built what I called my mini garden on my mini patio. But it wasn't [a patio], it was a fire escape, which gave it a bit more charm, I guess. . . . I found myself working on my garden for hours at a time, pruning, harvesting the fruits of my encouragement given by my beautiful plants growing. While Bob Marley sang his songs from my speakers overflowing to the streets, I gazed down and looked at the awe from passersby. They would look up, like a daisy rapidly growing towards the sun, and smile while to their surprise a flower would already be spiraling on its way down. Turning and looking down the street I would see people pointing and smiling, while I . . . [ate] some new strawberries growing profusely over the side of its container. . . .

I sat out there happy sightseeing and thinking of what my life would be like and how I wanted to live it. I looked around and said to myself, "I want to be a farmer . . . a farmer in the city." I looked over at my roommate Rich, and we both with bright eyes began to say that we are Urban Farmers. . . . Then I said, "Look at that roof—there is nothing but blacktop. There are so many rooftops empty and unused, deteriorating with roof rot and neglect. Imagine if there were a farm on each."

Today, Urban Farmers is dedicated to cultivating sustainable environments in metropolitan and urban areas. Their mission is to create year-round farms in economically neglected neighborhoods—reconnecting people with the environment, providing an extra source of income, providing an extra source of organic nutrition and creating a culturally stable community with a foundation based in healthy living and constructive growth.

Game-changing indeed! But Noah didn't stop there. He sees his passion for growth not just in plants, but also in people. "As humans, we must also have growth in our life. It is a fundamental thing for people to have some sort of growth tool so they can bear the fruit of their excellence. With Dream Talks, I've created a way for people to become who they want to be and to achieve what they want in life using technology."

Noah started Dream Talks as a way to get people from all walks of life thinking about their dreams and to give them the tools for creating change in their lives. He is working to bring his program to schools as part of their curriculum because he believes that following one's dreams is equally as important as math and science. Dream Talks works with kids and their families, showing them how different paths can lead to their dreams. Many children don't get support to follow careers outside of traditional paths (for example, doctor, lawyer, nurse, teacher) because their parents don't think those paths will lead to success. By participating in the program, parents learn the value of various careers.

I came to deeply understand the importance of Noah's work when I spent time with a fifty-year-old architect who was weeping over the lost opportunity of not being able to do what he loves. His true passion has always been interior design, but he never pursued that passion because his family had a negative perception of men in that field. In essence, Noah is educating communities, one family at a time, about what is possible when we follow our dreams and passions. These tiny changes are creating a seismic cultural shift that will move our world forward.

MULTIPLE PASSION POINTS
From Marketing to Matchmaking

Game Changers like Noah Graj infuse a singular passion into everything they do. But others find ways to connect various, sometimes unrelated, passions into one amazing lifestyle. My life offers a trifecta of passion points: I love solving problems, I love bringing stories to life and I love connecting people. I'm always seeking opportunities to connect these seemingly disparate worlds.

My early career in satellite engineering and deep space science was all about solving problems. At PanAmSat, I had the rare opportunity to transition satellite PAS5 to PAS9. I was entrusted with developing the contingency plan for transitioning clients who used the satellite to different channels in case of a catastrophic failure. It was a massive undertaking. Military operations, TV stations, medical devices, financial operations and millions of phone users that utilized the satellite airspace would lose their signal if anything went wrong. I loved the challenge, and after a successful transition, the team felt such a great sense of accomplishment.

Through my company Next Galaxy Media, I help clients like Coca-Cola and Microsoft Xbox solve their marketing challenges by bringing their company and product stories to life. If you think about it, storytelling is the essence of marketing. The technology I employ in reaching and engaging my customer's customers varies—be it satellite, Internet, radio or TV—but the goal is always to tell a powerful story that resonates with people.

I'm also passionate about connecting people. As far back as high school I regularly set my classmates up with one another. I even got in big trouble once for writing a love letter for a guy to give his girlfriend. (My teacher, who happened to be a nun, got ahold of the letter. Let's just say my knuckles still turn white at the sight of a ruler.) Later, I put myself through engineering school working as a matchmaker. Today, I own One2One, an event-driven online dating website, mobile app and magazine. We help singles find compatible "activity partners"—people who enjoy doing the same activities they do, whether it's going to a movie or concert or learning to play golf. Some people even find love!

Transitioning from a career in deep space science to dating, some people thought I was crazy. They often asked how I went from working for SETI (Search for Extraterrestrial Intelligence) to the online dating industry. I joke that the mission is the same—looking for intelligent life-forms! But instead of helping beings connect and communicate in outer space, I'm doing it right here on earth.

The common thread through everything I've done has been to align my work with my passions. But that didn't happen by luck.

Creating a passion-driven lifestyle doesn't fall into your lap. It takes a lot of blood, sweat and, yes, even tears on occasion. But it is well worth the effort, as I can honestly say that my work fills me with joy each and every day.

FIND YOUR RADICAL PASSION

- **DON'T CONFUSE WHAT YOU LOVE TO DO WITH WHAT YOU ARE RADICALLY PASSIONATE ABOUT.** I love to dance, but I am not willing to practice 24/7 or exercise the discipline required to train to be a game-changing dancer, and that's the first clue that I am not radically passionate about dancing. You can only be a category of one in an area that you are relentlessly passionate about.

- **EXPRESS YOUR PASSION DAILY.** Live your passion in the context of everyday life until it becomes second nature and a way of life. I am forever helping people with their technical problems; my friends know I love to brainstorm and find solutions to problems, so they call me whenever they have a new idea or a challenge. This is no different from the work I do with clients such as Coca-Cola, or what I was doing at Boeing, coming up with new, innovative technical solutions to everyday problems.

- **TURN YOUR PASSION INTO A CAREER.** Start by joining an association or club that focuses on your passion. This will give you access to other enthusiastic people in the industry so that you can learn the ropes of breaking into that field. Talk to executives and entrepreneurs whose work interests you. One good resource is SCORE, a nonprofit organization that puts retired executives and entrepreneurs in touch with people who need their advice.

- **DON'T DOUBT YOUR INSTINCTS.** Don't discard your gut feelings and instincts. With time, you will develop the vocabulary and be able to put voice to what you are thinking. This phase often causes people to doubt themselves. For example, I remember seeing content that I knew was off, but I couldn't put my finger on why. I would think, "This looks like crap," and the experts would look at it and instantly indicate, "This is out of phase." I now have the expertise to precisely state what my instinct sees.

PASSION KEEPS THE FLAME BURNING

Passion is the spark that starts the fire of change, and it is also the fuel that keeps the fire burning. Passion is energizing—it will power you forward when you are so exhausted you think you can't possibly go on. Passion drives courage, providing the mettle and resolve to overcome the obstacles and challenges that will inevitably arise on your journey. And finally, passion magnifies your skills and abilities, giving you the confidence to take on ever-bigger challenges. For every ailment, passion is the answer, the cure.

Passion Is Energizing

To break through to uncommon success, Game Changers must live, breathe, sleep and eat their work. No one achieves greatness without incredible amounts of hard work. There are going to be days when you don't feel like doing what needs to be done. Passion energizes you, excites you, makes you feel alive. It is passion that sees you through the long hours and inevitable challenges.

Mike Gallagher is a game-changing entrepreneur in the telecommunications industry. "There are some days when it's really hard to get yourself motivated. If you're not passionate about something, you're not going to be able to get yourself in the game. You have to identify that passion, whether it's being passionate about a product you think the world really needs or providing jobs for a hundred people to feed their families. You have to really think you're changing the world in some way. That's what I needed. I actually believed we were doing good in the world by helping companies and people out."

A Game Changer's life is centered on what excites and energizes them, and that is the reason they can outwork everyone else. Doing what I love has allowed me to consistently go the extra mile. I can recall many moments of boundless energy working in the center of my passions. My company worked with Universal Music to produce a documentary called *The Psychology of Mary J. Blige.* I remember waking up in the middle of the night with utter excitement, writing down ideas for how to bring Mary J.'s story to life. And it was passion that fueled all-nighters of sorting through and editing thousands of photos and videos.

At PanAmSat, passion was my motivation to go above and beyond. I volunteered to work weekends, always looking for opportunities to solve problems. I worked late many nights, building internal tools to make our work easier. I wasn't getting paid for it; in fact, no one knew how much time I was spending on these other projects. But I felt it was a privilege to have such a fantastic job doing what I truly enjoyed.

You've got to do what you love, because only true passion can carry you through those times when your legs and sheer willpower can't.

Passion Drives Courage

Passion creates courage and the drive to move forward even in the face of fear, uncertainty and seemingly insurmountable odds. Nelson Mandela exemplifies the courage that passion can generate. He was so passionate about freedom and ending injustice that he was willing to die for it. On trial for sabotage and facing the death penalty, Mandela said to the court: "I have fought against white domination, and I have fought against black domination. I have cherished the ideal of a democratic and free society in which all persons live together in harmony and with equal opportunities. It is an ideal which I hope to live for and to achieve. But if needs be, it is an ideal for which I am prepared to die." He was spared the death penalty but sentenced to life in prison. After twenty-seven years in prison (during which he was offered conditional release three times), he was freed. That is the power of passion!

Passion allows us to give of ourselves with reckless abandon, unafraid of the consequences or judgment. Passion says yes when everything and everyone else says no. When I came to America from Ghana as a teenager, I had a heavy accent and the kids at school ridiculed me. Speaking in front of others became a source of pain. But I had a passion for communicating that outweighed the shame I felt. Passion gave me the courage to step outside my comfort zone. Passion gave me the courage to become a university senator at Syracuse and ultimately to become a speaker, giving presentations to audiences of thousands.

Passion Magnifies Your Skills

Passion is an irresistible force that attracts like a powerful magnet the opportunities and circumstances to grow and share your talents and skills. "Outlaw" micro–race car driver Sara Elrod has defied the odds racing as a woman. Sara shared with me, "Even before I started racing, I always wanted to go faster driving a golf cart around my grandparent's house. I was always driving something. When I was five, my dad took me to a dirt track and asked me if I wanted to start junior racing. I had a car a few months later and started racing the next year when I was six. I definitely remember my first drive when I wanted to keep going fast!"

Dr. Patricia Bath, a pioneer in the field of ophthalmology, is another game-changing woman. "Having gifted hands for ophthalmic microsurgery is a blessing. I consider my surgical skills God-given in the same way that someone has a gifted voice, gifted artistry or Olympic-winning athleticism. Certainly, knowledge, practice and training are necessary; however, I believe to be able to perform at the level of excellence is a gift. When I discovered I had surgical skills, I became passionate about doing surgery." Dr. Bath's invention and surgical procedure have restored sight to people who had been blind for years.

Passion is an essential game-changing trait. It is the "secret sauce"—the key ingredient—of being a Game Changer. When you find your passion and pursue it relentlessly, you become a "category of one." There is no competition. You will discover how to find your passion—your inner spark—in Part Two. For now, start dreaming . . . imagining . . . and listening for the whisper of your passion calling you to be more.

Active Compassion

We make a living by what we get, but we make a life by what we give.

- WINSTON CHURCHILL -

 Several years ago, I went back to Ghana for my father's funeral. In Ghana it is customary to have ceremonial cloth specifically created for various occasions. An older gentleman at the funeral wore a cloth with two hearts facing each other, one on top of the other. I was familiar with the heart, or *Akoma*, as it's known in the Akan language of West Africa, but hadn't seen it in this configuration.

When I asked the gentleman what the symbol represented, he said, "Compassion." He went on to explain that the top heart represents the window through which we see the world with love. The bottom heart turned upside down becomes "balls"—the audacity to express love by taking action on another's behalf. Compassion, he said, is twofold: the heart to love and the balls to respond! Compassion is love in action.

The gentleman then told me that he had chosen this particular cloth because he felt it encapsulated the eighty years my father spent on earth fighting against social injustice and giving a voice to the voiceless. My father lived a life of compassionate service. He initially wanted to be a Catholic priest, but was forced to leave the priesthood after his father died and he had to help take care of his family. He later became an attorney with the Catholic Church and Amnesty International and worked tirelessly to help start the New Patriotic Party to restore Ghana to a democratic country. Compassion was the cornerstone of my father's life. It was the source of his love for people and his courage to fight for their freedom.

I realized a few more things about compassion in those precious moments I spent with my father's old friend. First was that the orientation, or direction, of love dictates passion and compassion. Passion is the inward expression of love; compassion is the outward expression of love. Both are twofold processes of understanding and taking action.

I also realized that compassion doesn't just happen; it's a conscious path that must be stalked. Compassion isn't just an emotion; it requires dedicated, unswerving action. In order to make an impact on the world, we must affect the lives of others in a positive way. A doctor who discovers a cure for a disease but doesn't share it, a comedian who can only make himself laugh or an artist who paints only for herself—these people are not Game Changers. Changing the game evolves humanity in some way. I believe that compassion is the next frontier for deep exploration, because within it lies our greatest hope for humanity.

LOVE IS THE CORE OF COMPASSION

As a matchmaker and founder of an online dating service, people often ask me my definition of love. I used to think I understood love, but it wasn't until my son was born that I was able to fully conceptualize love and break it into its elemental bits. In its purest form, love is wanting another person to be at their highest and best state of being—happiness. If I love another person, I want that person to be happy. I feel a great sense of accomplishment and satisfaction from bringing this person joy and easing their pain. Seeing this person happy automatically makes me happy and fulfilled.

Once I understood love in those terms, I started recognizing it everywhere. I realized at a deep level how truly simple it is to love others—no matter their race, religion, creed or past or present circumstances. All human needs fall into one of two categories: racing toward joy or escaping from pain (which leads back to happiness). Once we understand that we are all seeking the same thing—happiness—we can find common ground and greater understanding of our journeys.

Seeing others through the window of love allows us to humanize them and their journey. Love opens the door to understanding and empathy. And with greater understanding and empathy comes greater compassion. With love comes the need to protect and advance others. In essence, life runs on love. Love is like a cosmic wi-fi that allows us to access and share one another's strengths and help heal our needs.

Game Changers tend to be deeply compassionate. They are great lovers of people who internalize the troubles and pains of others. With understanding, empathy and ultimately love, they are radically passionate about helping other people solve problems, escape pain and move toward greater joy. That is why they are so often able to evolve humanity itself—they understand the great needs of the world and become committed to solving them.

To unlock greater compassion, love others by first seeking to understand them—their pains, problems, needs and challenges. See others through the lens of empathy, without judgment. Seek the common ground on which you both stand—the desire for happiness in life. If you come from a place of understanding and empathy, compassion is easily activated. When you seek to bring joy and happiness to others, you find happiness and fulfillment yourself.

ACTION IS THE PRECURSOR TO GREAT CHANGE

While love is at the core of compassion, love without action is just a warm fuzzy thought. Compassion is not only seeing the potential path to joy for another, but actively doing something to help them achieve it. Indifference and inaction are as insidious as hate. Active compassion asks, "How are you going to heal another's hurt? What are you going to do to bring others joy? What action are you going to take to contribute to the world?" Compassion goes beyond love. It's about making an impact, making a real difference in your own life, your community, our world.

For several years I lived a double life as a deep space scientist by day and a matchmaker by night. I kept my dating business on the side until the day I read a news story about how America had gone from being married with children to being home alone. It was a problem that I understood firsthand and that many of my friends were also struggling with. About the same time, I came across a census report indicating a continuing decline in marriage and increase in divorce. (This was part of my obsessive focus to gain a native understanding of the dating business.) Between escalating divorce rates, people delaying marriage and the massive growth of technology, we had become a land of lonely, disconnected people. Even worse, these forces are affecting our communities as the family nucleus breaks down.

This information was the straw that broke the camel's back. I knew I had to take action. I wanted to heal this hurt that was close to my own heart. So I made the decision to leave my secure job with Boeing and start *One2One*, a high-end magazine dedicated to singles. When I left my job at Boeing, some people suggested that I was wasting my talent by going into the dating business. But from my perspective, helping the fight against loneliness and escalating divorce rates is just as important as curing any of the many ailments in our world. Wherever there is a need and you can fill that need, you are taking compassionate action.

Within a short time, *One2One* was named one of the top ten new magazines of the year by Amazon, outranking magazines launched by mega-media companies. The award was gratifying, but I knew there was still more work to be done, more problems to solve. As a single myself, I empathized with the hurt singles often endure in certain situations. There's nothing quite as embarrassing as hearing your name called over the loudspeaker at a restaurant: "Spio, party of one." All eyes turn to you, making you feel even more self-conscious than you already did. I began researching and collecting information about ways to make social situations easier for singles, including travel for singles and restaurants with single-friendly seating. *One2One* has since introduced the notion of "single-friendly venues" to business establishments around the country to help make them more enjoyable for solo patrons.

While working as a matchmaker, I also had discovered that busy single professionals would often forgo doing the things they loved to do (concerts, sporting events, fine dining and so on) if they didn't have anyone to do them with. They were waiting for a love relationship in order to start living a fulfilling life. So I launched One2One.com—a lifestyle app that allows people to find others wanting to do the things that they don't want to do by themselves. I continue to make it my mission to create tools and resources to bring singles together and help them find love and happiness.

Through compassion for others, Game Changers identify the problems and fill the gaps that no one else is addressing. That compassion comes in flavors as diverse as the number of people on earth. My compassion is directed toward singles and Game Changers in the making. Dr. Patricia Bath's compassion is directed toward the blind.

While an ophthalmology fellow at Columbia University, Dr. Bath discovered that African Americans were twice as likely to suffer from blindness and eight times more likely to develop glaucoma. This understanding led her to develop a community ophthalmology system to increase the amount of eye care for those unable to afford treatment. She also cofounded the American Institute for the Prevention of Blindness, which established that "eyesight is a basic human right." Dr. Bath is perhaps best known for her invention of the Laserphaco Probe, which utilizes laser technology for a less painful and more precise treatment of cataracts. With her Laserphaco Probe, she was able to help restore the sight of individuals who had been blind for more than thirty years.

Dr. Bath shared with me the source of her compassion. "My brother Rupert and I were born to a dream seeker from the South and a dream-chasing immigrant from Trinidad who fell in love in New York. Although we lived in Harlem and were considered poor, my brother and I grew up thinking we were rich. It's amazing how a strong family anchor in love can instill a rich self-confidence, unconquerable strength and irrevocable hope. My brother and I believed that we could achieve whatever we dreamed with education, hard work and perseverance.

"There was also a great love of humanity in the Bath family household, which provided inspiration to study medicine," she continued. "Compassion was and remains my raison d'être. My first desires to become a physician were driven by the need to heal, to care for and to treat the sick. I wanted to save humanity and cure those crippled by disease like my childhood hero, Dr. Albert Schweitzer. While a medical student at Howard University, I was exposed to master teachers who encouraged me to pursue excellence and greatness, not because of ego, but because of the benefit to mankind. The compassion and love demonstrated towards patients by my mentors, Dr. Lois Young and Dr. LaSalle Leffall, did more than just teach. It became embedded within me."

Compassion is a game-changing trait. Love paired with action can achieve what no amount of money or talent alone can accomplish. Look at many of the great Game Changers throughout history—Mother Teresa, Abraham Lincoln, Louis Pasteur—and you will see active compassion.

ONE PERSON WITH COMPASSION
CAN CHANGE THE WORLD

The entire world is symbiotic. Whether we realize it or not, we are all connected in one way or another. We are all on the same ship together. No matter where one is sitting—first class or economy—if the ship goes down, we all perish. Some people think, "If a situation or event doesn't affect me, why should I bother? I have my own problems to contend with." Because when we mute the voices of those in pain, we hurt ourselves. When we turn a deaf ear or blind eye, we miss the opportunity for positive change. We have the chance in an increasingly connected world to truly get to know each other and search for solutions to help each other in our journey to joy.

The interdependence of our world requires each of our contributions. Game-changing inventions and innovations can come from people in all stations of life and every corner of the world. Greatness is not limited to a chosen few; it is not an anomaly that pops up every now and then. Greatness exists within each and every person on the planet. Massive change happens when we each take action. The little ways in which we all can be Game Changers lead to big ripples that can change and improve humanity. History has proven time and time again that one person literally can change the world. Jessica Jackley is a case in point.

Jessica is the cofounder, along with her ex-husband Matthew Flannery, of Kiva, a nonprofit organization that operates an online lending platform that allows individuals in the developed world to make microloans to budding entrepreneurs in the developing world. Kiva, which comes from the Swahili word for *unity*, was born out of pure compassion. Jessica indicates in a TED Talk that she has wanted to help others since age six. "I was very eager to be useful in the world—I think we all have that feeling."

But it was a speech by Dr. Muhammad Yunus on microfinance and helping the poor that became the call to action that altered the course of Jessica's life. In an interview with Mixergy, Jessica said, "[Hearing Dr. Yunus] just changed something for me, and I was so compelled that I quit my job a few weeks later and went to East Africa to learn about this microfinance thing myself."

Matthew and Jessica decided to combine his technical background and her big heart and microfinancing knowledge into the Internet-based Kiva.org. Kiva lenders have financed small business people around the world, including a spinach farmer in Cambodia, a hot dog stand man in Nicaragua, a carpenter in Gaza, a beekeeper in Ghana, a fish seller in Uganda, a seamstress in Paraguay, a cobbler in Kenya and a cattle farmer in Tajikistan. Since Kiva's founding, more than 1.1 million lenders have loaned more than half a billion U.S. dollars to more than 1.2 million entrepreneurs in seventy-six countries.

In an interview with Stanford University's Graduate School of Business, Jessica describes the game-changing philosophy of Kiva in one simple sentence: "Kiva reframes stories of poverty into stories of entrepreneurship." She went on to say, "I admire the very underprivileged entrepreneurs I've met all around the world who make amazing things happen in their own lives. One gentleman, Patrick in northern Uganda, has a very sad story, of course: He needed to survive and literally rolled up his sleeves and dug his hands into the dirt and made that dirt into clay. He borrowed enough money to buy matches and build a kiln so he can make bricks. Now he has a handful of employees."

That is the awesome power of a compassionate Game Changer!

Jessica started a small ripple that is now creating Game Changers in every corner of the globe. The entrepreneurs financed through Kiva are able to not only improve their own lives, but also positively impact their neighbors and communities. Jessica Jackley is one individual who has enriched the lives of millions of people she will never even know.

Active compassion is at the heart of Noah Graj's life as well. "I have always felt the desire, the need and the obligation to take what I have been given and have a positive effect on the world. And that's really the big driver for me—to be able to look back at my life and say that I gave people something they didn't have before, that I created communities and helped create processes that began to fundamentally change how we think and act. I am one who is always looking for the next way for us to change how we do business, how we interact with people and how we benefit each other's humanity."

ACTIVATE YOUR COMPASSION

- **TAKE ACTION.** Reach out to solve a problem for a stranger. The news is replete with things going wrong in the world, and that's a great place to scout for opportunities to exercise compassion. Life and business are all human endeavors, and Game Changers are problem solvers. Purpose plus passion creates power.

- **CONNECT WITH OTHERS.** Talk to people. Ask questions. There's something to learn from everyone you meet, and you never know what might come of it. Years ago, a casual conversation between two strangers on an airplane resulted in a game-changing innovation. C. R. Smith, then president of American Airlines, met R. Blair Smith, a senior sales representative for IBM, on a flight. Their conversation sparked an idea for a data-processing system that could create and manage airline seat reservations and instantly make that data available electronically to any agent at any location. Six years later, that airborne exchange of ideas became the first automated airline reservation system, now known as Sabre.

- **TRACE YOUR ANCESTRY.** I discovered talking to my father that our last name comes from Publius Cornelius Scipio Africanus (236–183 BC)—also known as Scipio the Great— the man who defeated Hannibal at Carthage and thereby changed Roman history. This nugget has given me a renewed interest in and a connection to Roman history. We are all connected in the human family, and understanding these connections increases awareness because as humans we are more keenly tuned to the pain of people who we have connections to.

- **ALWAYS ANSWER WITH HUMANITY.** The CEO of a major label once advised me, in a business meeting, "In every scenario, make sure you answer with humanity first—that everyone can connect to. Data has a tendency to get over people's heads, their eyes glaze over when they hear numbers first." This is a very useful insight. For example, one of the questions he asked me was, "How do you know that virtual reality technology is going to be the wave of the future?" Answering with data would entail simply stating the numbers. Answering with humanity, on the other hand, means pointing out that virtual reality is what people want because

they want their experiences delivered to them, and that pent-up demand is what has led 1.35 billion people to try virtual worlds.

COMPASSION IS THE DOORWAY TO OPPORTUNITY

Compassion is not a quality that people often equate with success. There is a misconception that compassion and success don't go together and that you have to be cutthroat in order to get ahead. This is a "lack and limitation" mind-set. The truth is that you can be a fierce competitor while also being compassionate. Great opportunity often hides in the situations and circumstances that make us angry or sad.

Another common fallacy about compassion is that it must be a charitable act—that compassion and profit can't or shouldn't coexist. Yet all businesses are examples of active compassion. They are charters of love, offering products and services that meet a need, solve a problem, alleviate some kind of pain or bring people joy. We often don't think of compassion in these terms, but in its basic form, compassion is seeing a problem and taking action to alleviate that problem. The most successful companies are the ones that best solve the biggest problems. That might be drilling for oil to keep us warm and fuel our cars, providing accommodations for weary travelers, manufacturing products that make life easier, making phones that help us stay connected, operating a twenty-four-hour drugstore that understands children always get sick in the middle of the night or even offering a cure for boredom such as video games.

Individuals and companies that successfully meet the needs of their customers get paid for helping people, and there's nothing wrong with that. A product, service, skill or talent—no matter how innovative or impressive—is useless if it offers no value to others. Businesses make a profit because they offer value by serving a significant need, want or desire for the greatest number of people. Compassion is not voided just because it's done for profit. We can do well by doing good.

Take for example a popular app called WhatsApp. WhatsApp started as a way for founder Jan Koum to post status updates on phones, and the original plan was to make it a paid app. But through compassion, it became something much, much more. Koum recently shared WhatsApp's story at a Mobile World Congress event.

> We can do well by doing good.

"There was a turning point when we realized we were actually onto something else here," he said. "I got an email from this girl who lived in Australia who was an exchange student . . . she said, 'I'm all by myself in Australia. I don't have any family here and it costs [too much] money for me to send them a message or call them. I cry myself to sleep because I'm all by myself.' I couldn't say no so I gave her a link [to the app] . . . and that's the moment when I realized we have a mission here of making sure people can communicate easily and affordably no matter where you are in the world and that's what we set out to do."

Knowing that international text messages can cost upward of $0.20 per text, computer whiz Koum came to the game-changing realization that SMS texts are simply data. Why not create an app that allows smartphone users to send each other text messages and images over the Internet at no cost? That's exactly what Koum and cofounder Brian Acton did, and WhatsApp morphed into a free international texting service. Koum and Acton solved a problem for millions of people that others had missed or ignored. With 450 million users worldwide, WhatsApp was bought by Facebook in February 2014 for $19 billion.

Game Changers understand that compassion is a key to unlocking opportunities. Through compassion and empathy for others, you can identify problems and fill voids that no one is addressing. It's all about understanding others' needs and providing relief. The more problems you can solve, the more you will be rewarded. Like Jan Koum and Brian Acton, former NBA star Earvin "Magic" Johnson has solved a lot of people's problems.

Many people talk about urban blight, but few step up and actually do something. Having experienced as a child the plight of the poor inner-city family, Johnson understands firsthand the needs and pains of those living in the neglected areas of America's largest cities. When Johnson looked at these communities, he saw people who were hungry for the basic dignities afforded others. In an interview with the *New York Times Magazine*, he recalled being told by a woman that there was nowhere near her home to buy salads. Most traditional companies either had completely ignored these communities because they feared them as poor thugs or had failed to operate successful businesses in these areas due to a lack of cultural sensitivity.

With obsessive focus, Johnson did his homework and made the economic case for development in these downtrodden communities. He recognized the enormous $500 billion spending power (at that time) of forty million African Americans. He also discovered that 25 percent of moviegoing audiences were African

American, and yet in predominantly African American neighborhoods, there were no movie theaters. And he pointed out that the
cost of land in these areas was less than half of what it was in more
affluent parts of town.

His compassion paid off, with Starbucks, TGI Fridays and
Loews Cineplex partnering with him to open locations in South
Central Los Angeles and Harlem, as well as disadvantaged communities in cities such as Atlanta, Houston and Cleveland. Many
other companies such as HMV, Disney and Old Navy have followed suit. Johnson insisted his partners make cultural adjust-
ments to reflect the needs and desires of the community. For
example, he understood that with limited funds, the concessions
that moviegoers purchased would often serve as dinner. Conse-
quently, his theaters are geared to sell more hot dogs than popcorn.
The Starbucks in these communities have also adapted culturally,
serving peach cobbler and sweet potato pie rather than croissant
sandwiches. The result? These movie theaters have some of the
highest-grossing concessions in the country, and many of the Starbucks stores are the most profitable in their respective cities.

Of giving people in these communities a place to meet, eat, be
entertained and feel whole, Magic said, "Man, I want to cry every
time I see that . . . *because they never had this before.*" He also
shared that when a job call at a theater in Harlem for one hundred
employees brought in five thousand applicants, he knew he had
impacted the community. He described the joy he felt on opening
day: "Just looking at those faces, the hope and pride, that may
have been the best moment of my life."

What most people saw as an area of blight, Magic Johnson saw
as a field of dreams. Through compassion, he found opportunity
and has amassed a net worth of half a billion dollars, making him

one of the richest athletes and African Americans. Not only has he changed the retail business game on many levels, but he has also changed the game for thousands of people living in inner-city communities. Healing the hurt always pays. It pays the heart, and it pays the bills.

Compassion is the cornerstone of great change. The world needs what I call mercy soldiers—armies of people taking compassionate action to make our world a better place, ridding it of fear, pain and isolation. We can truly do this through compassion—by consciously choosing to use our time, gifts and talents for good. The beauty is that when we serve others with compassion, we also serve ourselves.

———

I believe you have to be okay with large successes or failures. Who you are is not the sum of just what goes right or wrong.

—SANDRA SAVAGE, FOUNDER AND EXECUTIVE
DIRECTOR, BELOVED MINISTRIES INC.

Obsessive Focus

Concentrate all your thoughts upon the work at hand. The sun's rays do not burn until brought to a focus.

ALEXANDER GRAHAM BELL -

One of the key differences that sets Game Changers apart is obsessive focus. Not dedicated concentration or even steadfast single-mindedness, but fanatical focus. Obsessive focus is being willing to go deeper and farther and higher into your chosen area than anyone else. It is becoming so immersed in an area that it defies description or labels, where a new category has to be created just for you. For instance, when we say Einstein, people think relativity; Larry Page, search; Michael Jordan, basketball; Oprah, positive living.

That level of focus takes commitment, persistence and dedication. Ah, but the results! It is extreme focus that allows a laser to cut steel, water to eat its way through mountains and people like you to change the game. Obsessive focus is the key to unlocking your genius.

FOCUS ON WHERE YOU'RE GOING

Changing the game requires a clear vision, goal or purpose. You have to be clear about where you're going—the desired outcome or end result. Having a clear vision is critical because the mind is constantly seeking to feed our focus. This is why when you don't have a goal or vision or purpose, you feel lost. Your mind is searching for something to pursue. When you dedicate yourself to your dream or purpose, there is a peace of mind and calmness that comes with it. That focus brings a sense of order to your mind.

A clear vision, goal or purpose gives the mind something to focus on. When you're crystal clear about your vision and focus on that vision with intention, everything you experience is created in that context and starts to take shape around that vision. I like to think of it as a formula:

Destination + Obsessive Focus = Distinction

The destination is where you want to go—your vision, goal or passion. Obsessive focus is the movement of mind, body and purpose toward that goal. When these two elements are combined, the outcome can be phenomenal. Tencent is a powerful example of what can happen when obsessive focus is applied to a vision.

Founded in 1998, Tencent has become China's largest Internet service portal, with more than 650 million active users. Tencent provides value-added Internet, mobile and telecom services, providing users with one-stop online lifestyle services. In September 2013, just fifteen years after its inception, Tencent's market valuation was US$101 billion and its online advertising revenue alone reached $500 million, surpassing Google. Tencent achieved this remarkable growth by obsessively focusing on their vision.

On a recent trip to China, I had the opportunity to visit with some of Tencent's leaders, including Michael Zhu, CEO of Dachu Network, Tencent Inc. "Our vision is to be the most respected Internet company, and our mission is to enhance people's quality of life through Internet services. Our goal is to have a hundred-year Tencent brand."

I asked Michael what has been the key to Tencent changing the Internet game. "The most important factor has been obsessive focus—always holding on to one task, one vision, and continuing to improve. We adhere to the plan."

A testament to their level of focus, more than 50 percent of Tencent employees are research and development staff. "Our biggest challenge is that the market changes really fast and there are more and more competitors," Michael explained. "We spend lots of time studying our competitors' strategies. We spend even more time studying our customers—what they want and what they want to see from us."

The distinction formula holds true for individuals as well as businesses. After graduating from Syracuse, I had several job offers, but I had a passion to work in satellite communications. So I directed my focus to that area and went to grad school to study deep space science. I also had a goal to work for a company called PanAmSat. I had my eyes set on them from the time I was an undergrad. I focused on the company and learned everything I could about them. By the time I graduated with my master's, I think I knew more about the company than most people who worked for them. I turned down multiple job offers from other companies. I waited four months, obsessively focusing on my goal to work at

PanAmSat. My persistence and focus eventually paid off, and they decided to hire me. The job proved to be a great learning ground for me and ultimately led to my patented work in digital cinema with Boeing. Destination + Obsessive Focus = Distinction.

Our mind, our thoughts and our actions all move in the direction of our dominant focus. I spent time at NASCAR with highly respected racing agent Charlie Patterson. Charlie is the man who brought the likes of Tony Stewart and Ryan Newman to NASCAR. One of the things I learned during my time with him is that race car drivers are told not to look at the wall, because if that becomes their focus, they will eventually crash into the wall.

Sara Elrod, a race car driver who has been racing since the age of six, also spoke of this focus in our interview. When I asked what she thinks about while driving, she said she focuses on where she wants to go. "For the most part, I look at where I'm going—the next turn or the next point down the track. If I were to look at what is right in front me—like another car's bumper—then I'm going to hit somebody."

Game Changers are like race car drivers. They know where they are going and direct an intense focus on that single destination.

IF YOU CHASE TWO RABBITS, YOU END UP LOSING BOTH

There are many distractions in life that dilute our focus, especially in an always-connected, always-on world. And it often seems that as soon as we commit to pursue a specific vision or dream, countless opportunities, projects and offers come our way to divert our attention. Game Changers, however, learn to ignore these distractions and focus their thoughts and energy like a Jedi.

One of my favorite sayings is: "If you chase two rabbits, you end up losing both." There's another version: "When you try to ride two horses with one behind, you end up splitting your pants." Either way, the point is the same: You can't effectively do more than one thing at a time. If you try to focus on multiple endeavors, you will often end up doing none of them well. Game Changers focus on one thing and one thing only at a time. Once they have mastered their craft or achieved their breakthrough, then they move on to the next goal.

This singular focus seems obvious enough. But Game Changers know that obsessive focus is as much about ignoring distractions as it is concentrating on their vision. Steve Jobs once said, "People think focus means saying yes to the thing you've got to focus on. But that's not what it means at all. It means saying no to the hundred other good ideas that there are. You have to pick carefully. I'm actually as proud of the things we haven't done as the things we have done. Innovation is saying 'no' to a thousand things."

In 2014, Jan Koum and Brian Acton sold their technology, WhatsApp, to Facebook for a staggering $19 billion. Founded in 2009, just two years later WhatsApp was in the top twenty of all apps in the U.S. market. At one point during WhatsApp's meteoric rise, someone supposedly asked Koum why they weren't promoting their success to the press. "Marketing and press kick up dust," Koum reportedly replied. "It gets in your eye, and then you're not focusing on the product."

Focus forces choice.

Koum reminds us that we are constantly making choices in life. More choices often lead to less focus. In many ways, we are more limited by our freedom than by our limitations. The more focused you are, the simpler your choices become. Focus forces choice. Focusing on one vision or goal leads to clear choices even in the midst of distractions and chaos. Pick your rabbit and go get it!

NARROW YOUR FOCUS

Here are three steps to help you hone your focus. Repeat these steps and before you know it, focus becomes a habit, then an obsession, then a lifestyle, then a tradition and ultimately your legacy.

- SET PRIORITIES. Boiling the ocean is a fruitless exercise. You can't do everything. Force yourself to sit, clear distractions and focus on your goals. Choose the most important target and then break that goal into its elemental bits, focusing on one step at a time.

- FILTER DISTRACTIONS. Once you know what is most important, it is easier to say no to distractions. Do you watch an extra hour of TV or spend that hour writing your novel? Do you play three hours of video games or create your business plan? Focusing solely on your vision requires discipline, and it starts with breaking each day into the highest-priority tasks and discarding everything else that detracts from that goal.

- DEDICATE TIME TO YOUR PRIORITIES. Your life is the sum of your choices, decisions and actions. What you focus on hourly, daily, weekly and monthly is ultimately what you become. You only have twenty-four precious hours each day.

Fill them wisely, and with focus and purpose, to achieve your goals.

DEVELOP A NATIVE UNDERSTANDING

Obsessive focus involves gaining a mastery of one's craft. It means understanding a particular subject deeper and more intimately than anyone else. It is delving so deeply into the nooks and crannies of a subject that you internalize everything there is to know about that subject—the what, the how, the why. Obsessive focus is digging as deep as you can and then digging even deeper.

This level of mastery leads to what I refer to as native understanding—when you are immersed so fully in your endeavor that you become one with it. Natives to an area intrinsically know the language, culture, needs and sensitivities by virtue of being deeply implanted in the region. Eskimos, for example, are known to have hundreds of words to describe snow. They have a native understanding of every nuance and attribute of snow—something that's part of their daily lives. They look at snow and see differences that others can't.

Game Changers must develop a native understanding and become a tribesman of their target area. When they possess this "overstanding" of their area, they are able to detect nuances, connect dots and see novel connections previously unknown, unseen and unexperienced. Albert Einstein didn't just understand relativity; he had an intrinsic understanding of atoms. If you were to spend an afternoon with Larry Page, founder of Google, he could tell you in excruciating detail the limitless power and uses of search algorithms.

In the movie *Forrest Gump*, Forrest's friend Bubba talks about the myriad of ways to cook shrimp: "You can barbecue it, boil it, broil it, bake it, saute it. There's shrimp kabobs, shrimp creole, shrimp gumbo. Pan-fried, deep-fried, stir-fried. There's pineapple shrimp, lemon shrimp, coconut shrimp, pepper shrimp, shrimp soup, shrimp stew, shrimp salad, shrimp and potatoes, shrimp burger, shrimp sandwich . . ."

Now that's a native understanding of shrimp! It's a humorous example that highlights one of the many benefits of obsessive focus. The deeper you get into an area, the more creative you become about ways to create value in that arena. It is derivative intelligence generated by focus, meaning you derive other ways to express value based on new things that you learn. Mastery yields inspiration, which in turn yields game-changing ideas.

If you want to change the game, you must become a native of your passion by committing to your endeavor entirely. What does that look like? For starters, it means going to that place where the indigenous gather. That could be conferences, networking or support groups, classes, courses or workshops related to your field. Spending time with the natives of your industry, in a special place dedicated to that industry, exposes you to like-minded people who are on the same path and who share your vision.

Able-bodied Muslims are required to make at least one pilgrimage to Mecca during their lifetime. Every industry has its Mecca. When I say Nashville, you think of country music. Madison Avenue—advertising. Hollywood—movies. Silicon Valley—technology. Many Game Changers physically visit their industry Mecca. Starbucks CEO Howard Schultz immersed himself in coffee in Italy. Jessica Jackley moved to East Africa before founding microlending platform Kiva.org. Mark Zuckerberg went to Harvard like his idol Bill Gates. Olympic athletes often move to certain cities or specialized training camps to be around others who are also preparing for the Olympics. This allows them to focus on their sport 24/7 and to be around others who have the same goals, values and vision. Where is the Mecca of your industry?

In a commencement address to MIT, Dropbox CEO Drew Houston stressed the importance of spending time in your Mecca. "There's only one MIT. And there's only one Hollywood and only one Silicon Valley. This isn't a coincidence. For whatever you're doing, there's usually only one place where the top people go. You should go there. Don't settle for anywhere else. Meeting my heroes and learning from them gave me a huge advantage. Your heroes are part of your circle too—follow them."

When I decided to pursue online video delivery for the radio industry through my digital marketing company, Next Galaxy Media, I moved to New York City and worked in the offices of our biggest client, Emmis Communications. By immersing myself in their environment for a year, I acquired a mastery of radio station operations. With that level of understanding, I was able to spot the needs my company could fill, the problems we could solve and the value we could offer to the radio industry. As a result of that obsessive focus, we were able to quickly make iterations to our programs and sign more than two hundred radio stations to license our software.

I took the same immersive approach when I decided to go into the dating business. I spent an entire year gobbling up any and all research, data and information that I could find about the industry. I interviewed a lot of people in the dating ecosystem. I spoke to hundreds of singles, getting to know them and their needs. In the process, I gained a native understanding of the industry, so much so that I wrote a report on singles in America and their spending power. It was the first of its kind to look at singles as a unique demographic. I became known as a subject matter expert and was called upon by news outlets like *The Bill O'Reilly Show*, *USA Today*, *Oprah* and others to discuss the dating industry and my One2One project.

Become a native of your passion. Make it your daily obsession. Focus on it with the intensity of a laser. Immerse yourself in it until you become one with it. Pursue relentlessly and vigorously. If you want to change the game, you have to know that game better than anyone else.

FOCUS AMPLIFIES STRENGTHS

You're probably already familiar with the analogy comparing focus to a laser beam. But do you know the science behind the comparison?

The difference between a lightbulb and a laser is focus. Both are light sources, and light sources are made up of energy. The waves from a lightbulb are omnidirectional, meaning they spread in all directions. The waves interfere with each other—crests and troughs cancel each other out. In contrast, a laser's energy is concentrated in one direction. The waves are synchronized, so there is no interference. Crests sit on top of crests—strength on top of strength. The result is massive power that is a million times stronger than a lightbulb's wave. This is how laser beams can travel very long distances and are powerful enough to cut steel.

Passion, talents and our gifts are our fundamental energy sources. Everyone has talents and gifts, but without focus, that talent is diffused. Like the light from a bulb, it doesn't make much of an impact. But when we focus our talents and gifts in one direction toward our goal or vision, it's strength on top of strength. Focus amplifies all our abilities, and the results are powerful.

Talent alone doesn't lead to greatness. There are scores of extremely talented people who never achieve success. The difference between average and category of one is obsessive focus. It's the difference between hundreds of incredibly skilled basketball players whom we've never heard of and Michael Jordan or LeBron James. Game Changers focus their talents, passions and purpose like a laser and etch their mark on the world.

Relentless Hustle

Success is never owned, it is only rented; and the rent is due
every day.

- RORY VADEN -

When I started college at Syracuse University, there were about
one hundred freshman students in the engineering program. During orientation, the dean said that some students would not graduate with an engineering degree. (He was right.) He explained
that while all of us had the ability to complete the requirements
for the degree, not all of us would be willing to do what it would
take to earn it.

Throughout that first year, everyone complained about how
difficult the courses were. But only a handful of students showed
up for the free tutorials that the engineering department provided
on weekends. There were a few of us who were constant fixtures in
those Saturday sessions. While everyone else was sleeping in or out
enjoying college life, we were slogging through electromagnetics,
physics and C++ programming. Not coincidentally, by graduation, the regular weekend-session attendees were the ones vying
for the top positions in our graduating class, with many of the top
engineering firms outbidding one another for a chance to hire us.

The difference between us and the rest of the engineering graduates (and even those who dropped out of the program) was relentless hustle. We all possessed more or less equal talent and academic abilities. And without a doubt, the other engineering graduates worked hard. But those of us who attended the weekend sessions went beyond hard work. Plain ol' hard work is working nine to five or maybe eight to six. It's doing what you have to do—and maybe even doing it very well—but not much more. Relentless hustle is going beyond what others are willing to do. It's doing whatever it takes to change your circumstances. It's running and gunning until your vision becomes a reality, making it happen by any means necessary. And it's finding the strength to take one more step each time you're ready to quit.

Now, I don't mean to suggest that you should be a workaholic. Relentless hustle is about finding yourself and your passion in the context of everything that you do. Relentless hustle is an up-and-coming Oprah Winfrey looking for every opportunity to speak in front of an audience. It's a young Bill Gates learning to code and getting an internship as a high schooler. And it's Game Changer Alex Cameron working countless hours for free at a radio station to gain experience.

You can possess all the other traits for game-changing success, but without hustle your vision isn't going anywhere. In the end, it all comes down to a relentless pursuit of the dream. When I worked as a matchmaker, it always amazed me that many men would skip over some of the most beautiful and well-balanced women in the service. When I started asking why, they often said something like, "She looks like she's out of my league." These men would refuse to pursue what they desired. But a few men were willing to take a chance on a date with a woman they thought was "beyond their reach." These men often ended up with what they desired. Pursuit is the true indication of desire. Relentless hustle is proof of the desire for change.

GAME CHANGERS ARE DOERS, NOT DREAMERS

Wanting and wishing for something won't bring it to fruition. A dream alone is not enough. A dream without hustle is nothing more than a daydream, a simple fantasy. There's a big difference between wanting to change your world and making a real impact. Dreamers are not changers. Doers are changers. Game Changers do continually what others only do occasionally.

Laurie Clark is definitely a Game Changer. She has not only changed the trajectory of her family history, but also made her mark in the retail industry. When Laurie shared her story with me, I discovered that relentless hustle has been the key to her success. "I had a very humble upbringing and grew up with not much of anything. From a young age, I knew I didn't want to spend my life like that. I wanted to do more. So at age fourteen I began working at a YMCA, washing floors, painting, doing whatever they needed done. Around that time, I also started ice skating. I worked very hard at it, and the rink decided to sponsor me. Little by little, I became very successful and won a regional championship. That experience instilled in me the confidence that if you work incredibly hard at something, you will reap the rewards.

"I wanted to go to college and had to work hard to achieve that as well," she continued. "I was the first person in my family on either my mother's or father's side to ever go to college. I worked all the way through high school and then through college because I had to pay for my education. I got a little financial aid, but the rest I earned working in retail stores and tending bars (usually two jobs at a time)."

Laurie's relentless pursuit of her dreams continued after college. "When I started my career, I had that burning desire to strive and do well in my career. While my friends were having fun as young adults, I was setting milestones for myself. At twenty-two years old, I set a goal to reach a certain level before I turned twenty-five and to be a divisional manager before I turned thirty. I constantly pushed myself, setting goals and working hard to achieve them. That was what pushed me along. From the time I was a kid, I worked hard to get what I wanted to achieve . . . that's why I was painting and sweeping and washing bowls."

Laurie epitomizes relentless hustle, and that hustle has garnered remarkable success. She was the youngest divisional manager at both Lechmere and Staples, the youngest woman on the senior executive team at Staples, one of the first female vice presidents at Staples, and the first person Staples sent to Harvard Business School's executive business program. Her story shows us that greatness is found in the details of our daily choices. Achieving uncommon success is not a single discrete accomplishment, but rather daily choices and actions that ultimately determine what you accomplish. Daily choices become routines, routines become habits, habits become rituals, rituals become traditions, traditions become your legacy.

When relentless hustle becomes your daily choice, you will own your greatness. Yaron Galai, one of the founders of Quigo, a contextual advertising platform pioneer, was in the midst of closing a $6 million deal when he was called to service in the Israeli Navy Reserve. He took his mobile phone with him. On the final day of negotiations on the deal, Yaron participated via conference call from his post in the Gaza Strip. Fifteen minutes into the call, someone began firing on his troops. The shooting was so loud, the investor on the conference call thought someone at Yaron's location was playing video games in the background. Upon finding out that Yaron was under fire, the investor decided to opt out of such a dangerous investment. Yaron later managed to convince the investor, who proceeded with the deal under one condition— that Yaron relocate to the United States. He and his partners later sold Quigo for $363 million to AOL.

Some people talk about their big dreams but never take action toward making those dreams a reality. The difference between a dreamer and a doer is consistent action. When you clothe a dream in relentless hustle, the result is game-changing.

TALENT ALONE ISN'T ENOUGH

There is no substitute for talent. But without hustle, a funny thing happens to talent . . . nothing! Talent without hustle is like a nice car with no gas—it's going nowhere fast. There are loads of talented people in the world, but only those who exercise that talent have a chance to change the game.

Game Changers go to great lengths to make their talents count—applying their skills and gifts to create value. They become successful based on what they choose to do with their talents rather than who they naturally are. Harvard professor Dr. Harry Lewis observed firsthand this trait in both Bill Gates and Mark Zuckerberg: "[They] were extremely hardworking. These were guys who spent a lot of time getting better at what they were doing. They were practicing; they were doing things that involved the kind of repetition that really gave them a lot of their skills."

I once had the opportunity to sit in the sound booth at a Kenny Chesney concert in a massive arena. That was when I gained a genuine appreciation not just for his music, but also his story. I see Kenny Chesney as a Game Changer in the country music business—not simply because of the amazing success he has achieved, but because he has stayed true to himself and his music. He does country his way, choosing to celebrate life through his music rather than the typical "tears in the beer" theme of the traditional country stars who came before him.

Anyone who has ever seen Kenny perform can see that he has tremendous talent. But country music singers with incredible talent are a dime a dozen. Yet no other country musician has achieved the uncommon success that Kenny Chesney has. According to *Billboard* magazine, Chesney is the most fruitful country artist of the millennium. As of this writing, he has been named the Country Music Association's Entertainer of the Year eight times and has won a slew of other awards. Of his fifteen albums recorded to date (with thirty million copies sold worldwide), fourteen have been certified gold or platinum. He has produced more than thirty top ten singles on the U.S. Billboard Hot Country Song charts, twenty-four of which reached number one. His concerts have sold one million tickets for each of his past ten tours. And since 2000, he has had the most listened-to song on country radio nearly 10 percent of the time.

So what shot Kenny Chesney to superstardom? Kenny exemplifies many game-changing traits. His creativity and passion for his music are evident in the variety of his songs. After graduating from college with a degree in marketing, he moved to the Mecca of country music, Nashville, and focused intensely on his craft. He worked odd jobs in Nashville until he landed a gig as a songwriter and then later a record deal. The embodiment of tenacity, he spent years playing dive bars, often for as few as ten people. In an interview with Soundcheck, he spoke of the work ethic he developed from having to haul, set up and tear down rented equipment on his own for every gig, often spending hours to set up and play for just a few tips and a free dinner. That relentless hustle continues even today. Chesney recently told SouthFlorida.com, "That's the biggest misconception [about me]. For a guy who sings a lot of songs about not working, I'm working all the time."

In the end, Game Changers are those who are willing to keep their nose to the grindstone and work their fingers to the bone to make their talent count. Our gifts can be used as a tool for great change as long as we are willing to hustle.

GAME CHANGERS LOOK FOR PROBLEMS TO SOLVE . . . AND THEN SOLVE THEM

Game Changers are doers who seek out problems and find creative, innovative solutions for them. If we look behind every game-changing innovation, we see that they all solved some kind of problem or met some kind of need. Game Changers use their knowledge, skills and talents to solve problems, serve others and make a contribution . . . and are richly rewarded for it.

The most successful people and companies are the ones that solve the biggest problems. In an entrepreneurial session at Stanford University, Mark Zuckerberg advised entrepreneurs to go after problems of significance that are personally meaningful to them. "Do something that's fundamental," he said. "A lot of companies I see are operating on small problems. It's cool to want to be an entrepreneur. The problem is trying to build a company that solves a tangible problem. The most interesting thing is to operate on something fundamental on how humans [live]. It was fundamental for me. I feel this need really acutely."

While some game-changing innovations have global and societal implications, I believe anything that solves a problem for another human being is a humanitarian act and therefore an important contribution. In my work with radio stations through my digital marketing company, I recognized a void in the marketplace. Advertising dollars were shifting from all media areas to online, with radio and print taking the biggest hit. Every radio station I met with complained about their program directors having to do double the work because they had to create one set of programming for on-air radio and a second set of programming for their websites. No one else in the market was addressing this problem, so I decided to focus my attention on helping radio stations create an online presence using video.

Radio stations create content around the clock, much of which goes to waste at the end of the broadcast. We developed a platform to capture a video stream live and archive that content online for on-demand consumption. We also created software that uses on-air playlists to automatically create online channels of videos, thus eliminating the need for program directors to program twice. Our software created a new model for radio stations to easily show all their valuable on-air content (celebrity interviews, humorous DJ banter, news, etc.) on their websites. This was a massive triumph for our company. One station credited our online video platform as being directly responsible for growing its digital revenue from 1 to 21 percent.

Some game-changing innovations start as solutions to large-scale problems, like Zuckerberg's solution to loneliness, while others are targeted to specific markets, such as my online video solution for the radio industry. But some start out very simply as a solution to one person's challenge and are so valuable they are then scaled to the masses. Such was the genesis of both the Whats-App and HopStop apps. That was also the path to uncommon success for Jon Oringer.

A serial entrepreneur, Jon Oringer has started at least thirteen companies. Twelve failed. The thirteenth is now one of the largest stock media libraries in the world (with twenty-seven million images and counting) and Oringer is a billionaire. In his previous ventures, Oringer was frustrated by the lack of reasonably priced artwork and photographs for his marketing materials and websites. So he decided to start yet another company—Shutterstock—to sell stock photos at a price anyone could afford in a hassle-free, royalty-free environment.

Jon described Shutterstock's birth to *Inc.* magazine: "I started in 2003 by shooting 100,000 images—everything I could find—over about six months. I grabbed a Canon Digital Rebel, which was $800 at the time. I culled the images down to 30,000 and put them on the website. I needed to seed it somehow." What is especially fascinating about this story is that Jon is not a professional photographer. He could have said, "I'd love to start a site that sells royalty-free photographs, but I'm not a photographer and I don't have any photos." Instead of letting that big "but" stop him, he bought a camera and got to work. "I was doing everything myself. That was my way to learn," he said. "I needed photographers, so I became a photographer."

Talk about hustle! Think about all the talented and passionate photographers in the world, many more talented than Jon. But how many were willing to spend six months taking one hundred thousand photographs without any guarantee of a return? How many were willing to try something new? While everyone else played the rights-managed, photo-licensing game the old way, Jon decided to turn the industry on its head. Now bloggers, small businesses, even individuals can create amazing graphical products without having to shell out loads of money for high-quality images.

Jon's idea was game-changing not just for those looking for images, but also for artists and photographers wanting to monetize their artwork. He explained, "The big change that happened was when I started getting other photographers interested in contributing their own content. I turned my one contributor account into an entire upload system for anyone. I opened up Shutterstock to the entire world, and created a contributor community. Anyone could give stock photography a shot. I knew this leap could either put me out of business or create the perfect marketplace model. This kind of model had never been created before. This was an all-you-can-eat model on one side, and contributors on the other side that needed to get paid at the right rate per image."

Jon Oringer proves that you don't have to be an insider to change the game. In fact, Game Changers in a particular industry are often outsiders because they have the ability to see that industry with a fresh, new perspective. Their ideas are often so innovative that they seem outlandish at first . . . that's what makes them game changing! When *Inc.* asked Jon Oringer what is next for Shutterstock, he said, "We are expanding in a lot of different directions. . . . We continue to look for pain points for our customers or contributors." No doubt as long as Jon continues to look for problems to solve, he will continue to have uncommon success.

The world is full of problems to solve, needs to serve, pains to heal. Game Changers readily step up to the plate and address them.

CULTIVATE A HABIT OF RELENTLESS HUSTLE

- **REMEMBER THAT SUCCESS IS A SNOWBALL.** Achieving any goal requires taking a series of steps that adds up to one giant leap. By taking actions toward achieving your priorities each day, you start to do these things as second nature and the momentum builds to enable you to make quantum leaps. It's a beautiful thing when it all starts to come together.

- **WHEN YOU GO TO WAR, YOU TAKE ALL YOUR WEAPONS.** No experience is wasted. Your game-changing moments are going to draw from those unique experiences that are exclusive to you. My company has developed a unique virtual reality audio headset called Ceekars, which came about because I looked at the gaming landscape and saw that a gap existed for people like me who enjoy games, movies and concerts but not on gaming consoles. I was able to lead the efforts for the development of this audio headset that works on any computer or mobile device because (a) in my electrical engineering classes way back when, I had worked on sound filters, so I understood the process, (b) as a 3D and immersive experience alphageek, I knew what I wanted my audio to taste and feel like, and (c) through my various endeavors, I built the connections to quickly put together the teams and tools needed to take advantage of this gap in the industry.

- **LEAD WITH PASSION.** Always be on the lookout for problems that need to be solved, needs that need to be served, pains that need to be healed—and start by looking where your passion lives.

- **CREATE VALUE WITH YOUR GIFTS AND SKILLS.** Find opportunities to get paid for what you love to do. This will help you hone your skills. Try starting with freelance sites like Fiverr.com, Elance.com and oDesk.com, where employers are seeking individuals with skills that you might have.

GAME CHANGERS DON'T WAIT FOR THE GAME TO COME TO THEM

Game Changers realize that success isn't handed to anyone. They make their own luck and create their own opportunities rather than waiting for them to show up on their doorstep. Relentless hustle is working your butt off 24/7 to have luck come your way. "A lot of people say luck plays a role in success," Marc Parker told me. "But if you really look at luck, it's what happens when you end up at the right place at the right time. But you put yourself there by taking the steps and doing the work and having the perseverance to get to that place."

Game Changers like Mike Gallagher make their own luck by creating the game rather than waiting for the game to come to them. In the 1990s, only the largest companies had access to broadband. When the Telecom Act of 1996 was enacted, Mike saw his chance to bring broadband to the masses. His founding of Florida Digital Network is a real David and Goliath story.

"The Telecom Act of 1996 mandated that monopoly phone

companies like Bell South and AT&T open their networks so that other providers would have access," Mike told me. "We knew what the law gave us the rights to do, so we forced the phone companies to give us space. We were the first people to put broadband across that network."

"We picked the largest cities in Florida and identified the classes of businesses that were eventual targets for broadband. Then we built a network that would reach 90 percent of those businesses," he continued. "We were gambling that there would be a market. There was no market for broadband internet in 1997. But we guessed that if people were using their phone lines and paying AOL for dialup, they would pay us for an always-on, faster connection. We took the chance that if we built it, there would be a market."

Mike and his team exhibited the relentless hustle that unlocks fortune's door. "We had a direct sales force that would literally go knock on doors and say, 'How about you fire your existing monopoly phone company and give us a chance?' And because we were the first company to offer an alternative, we were very well received. People wanted something different, and we were that alternative."

Find the opportunity and work tirelessly, and you will create your own luck.

Mike Gallagher didn't wait for the game to come to him. He had the hustle to seek out a problem and the drive to find an innovative solution and completely changed the broadband industry. Going up against billion-dollar phone company monopolies, he started Florida Digital Network from zero and later sold it for a quarter of a billion dollars.

Luck, timing, fate—call it what you may—it is the magic that happens when opportunity meets hustle. Find the opportunity and work tirelessly, and you will create your own luck. Game-changing success requires not money, privilege, talent or luck, but the relentless pursuit of a vision. Uncommon success is found in the pool of giant sweat drops that roll off the brow of those who hustle relentlessly.

Don't take no for an answer. When we tried to get the wheels made for our neutron bike, every place we went, people said, "That can't be done." We kept on because we knew there was a way to do it. Everybody is going to tell you, "That can't be done. Don't even try it. Don't waste your time." Don't listen to that! If you know you're doing the right thing, just keep moving forward.

—SHANON PARKER,
PARKER BROTHERS CONCEPTS

The difference between people who make it and those who don't is that the people who make it figure out ways to overcome obstacles. Everybody out there is going to try and pull you down. You've got to think, "I believe this is right. Just because it hasn't been done this way doesn't mean it's wrong. It just means it hasn't been done." If you believe in it strong enough, nobody can stop you but you.

—MARC PARKER,
PARKER BROTHERS CONCEPTS

Extreme Audacity

If you're not doing some things that are crazy, then you're doing
the wrong things.

- LARRY PAGE, GOOGLE FOUNDER -

Game Changers are bold, daring and adventurous. In a word,
they are audacious—unafraid to take risks, to push the boundaries of what's possible and to constantly question the status quo. It
takes extreme audacity to defy the norm, to break through others'
limiting beliefs, to do what no one else believes you can do. The
audacious Game Changer doesn't take no for an answer. Just ask
Dr. Patricia Bath.

Dr. Bath has changed the game repeatedly throughout her life.
Her bio is full of firsts: the first African American to complete a
residency in ophthalmology (1973); the first female faculty member
in the Department of Ophthalmology at UCLA's Jules Stein Eye
Institute (1975); the first woman to chair an ophthalmology residency training program (1983); the first African American female
doctor to receive a medical patent (1988). She shares her story:

> The audacity I have had since childhood has carried me as my
> default strategy. As a fifth- or sixth-grade student, I had the au-

dacity to believe I could become a physician. Then, at the age of fifteen, as a National Science Foundation summer fellowship student, I had the confidence and audacity to believe my experiments would work.

Later, in my early research on laser cataract surgery, I recall being told by the institute director, "Who are you to think you can execute that experiment?" That was my first hurdle to success, because at that point in time, I had no credentials as a laser scientist. I was only a laser scientist wannabe. My second hurdle was the fact that I didn't have a grant and was in a foreign country (Germany). And the third hurdle was that my idea was so new that I was faced with incredulity by the super-brilliant and knowledgeable professor that I needed to convince.

In spite of all these hurdles, the fact that I had the outrageous audacity to stand ramrod straight and argue my case without the blink of an eye convinced the professor that I should be given a chance. He finally agreed that it was such a brilliant idea that I should be allowed to have a few weeks' use of lab facilities, even though I didn't have a grant and he was skeptical it would work. After three to five weeks of grueling twelve-to-eighteen-hour work days, I had proven the feasibility of my idea and had the data to publish and the evidence of success. I filed for my patent in 1986 and shared my discovery with the scientific community in 1987.

I love Dr. Bath's story because it so beautifully illustrates the audacity that all Game Changers possess. It's not enough to exercise creativity and be passionate about one's idea. To change the game, one must have absolute unyielding conviction and belief in that idea. Being the scientist that I am, I think of the formula for audacity as one part courage plus one part boldness. Game Changers must have the courage to take the unknown path, even in the face of fear, and to confront skepticism and judgment. Just as important, they must also be bold enough to take the risks that ultimately redefine convention.

COURAGE IN THE FACE OF FEAR

A key difference between those who achieve some measure of success and those who achieve truly uncommon success is courage. Without courage, fear stops us from taking action. When I was a cadet in the air force, I had a rare opportunity to fly at negative g-force in an air force T37. I was filled with pure, unadulterated fear to the point of intestinal upheaval. (Yes, I vomited!) I quickly opted out of the exercise. As I walked away from the group, the pilot yelled out, "Failure Expected And Received, Cadet Spio . . . FEAR!"

I stopped in my tracks, turned around and went back. The pilot shared the safety record of the training exercise, including the fact that no cadet had ever died. He assured me of our success as a team and said, "Now, are you Feeling Excited And Ready? That's FEAR too, but used in a wise way."

I summoned all my courage and decided to go for it. After the flight, I asked about taking flying lessons. The pilot said, "Now we're talking! That's what I call intestinal fortitude!"

That was an amazing lesson for me in so many ways. For starters, I learned that excitement and fear often have the same symptoms. And I almost walked away from a great experience because of my False Expectations About Reality (another FEAR acronym).

It also taught me that most of the time, our fears are imagined rather than real.

For thousands of years, fear was a necessary tool that warned us of very real physical danger. It was a primal instinct that helped us survive. In modern times, without saber-toothed tigers to contend with, that primal instinct is often directed toward psychological rather than physical danger. We fear failure, rejection, new situations, the unknown, even change itself.

Game Changers are not necessarily fearless. Rather, they consciously choose to not allow fear to dictate their future. They understand it's how we *respond* to fear that either makes or breaks us. "One of the fundamental truths that has helped me was learning to recognize that fear is really my own creation," said Dream Talker and Urban Farmer Noah Graj. "Now I recognize what things I am doing to hold myself back as opposed to letting myself live. I understand that although I might have fears and insecurities, I still need to move forward."

That is the essence of courage—moving forward in spite of fear. Courage is not fearlessness, but rather acting in the face of fear. It takes courage to be a Game Changer, because it's all about leading the charge into the unknown. Courage breeds audacity by using fear wisely to gather knowledge and create excitement. Audacity confronts fear, embraces it and moves ahead anyway.

COURAGE IN THE FACE OF JUDGMENT

Recently I gave a speech to a group of students in Mexico. Afterward, an eleven-year-old girl came up and thanked me. When I asked what for, she said, "For making me believe that my dreams are not crazy or silly." She quietly admitted that one day she wants to become the president of Mexico, but she was ashamed to share this dream because she thought it was too far-fetched and crazy. After hearing my story, she developed the courage to go after that dream, and with me standing behind her, she shared her dream with the class.

Game Changers are often doubted, questioned and sometimes even ridiculed because their thinking and ideas are so outside the box, so different from what others consider to be possible. They quickly discover that putting themselves and their ideas out there for all to see and judge is a bridge that must be crossed.

It seems hard to imagine that technology like computers and smartphones, which are now part of our daily lives, were met with skepticism when first introduced. In my interview with Harvard professor Dr. Harry Lewis, he shared, "When Bill Gates started programming microcomputers, the faculty really didn't think they were anything more than toys. [Gates] had a willingness to take some risks on things that were not generally appreciated and probably met with a good degree of skepticism."

Noah Graj describes the importance of audacity and putting oneself squarely in the face of judgment. "Being audacious is about not being afraid to be different and do something different that hasn't been done before," he told me. "It's not being ashamed of living life on your own terms. People might not understand an idea at first, or it might not make sense to them at that time. You have to not be afraid of being ridiculed or called crazy."

Noah has a very nontraditional look. He wears long dread-locks, and people (particularly the CEOs he works with as a brand strategist) often have preconceived ideas of who he is until they get to know him. "For sixteen years I have been growing locked hair," he explained. "What inspired me to begin doing this was the real-ization that I was living within the confines of society and the desire to fit in. I realized I had been making decisions in fear of what others expected and wanted of me, instead of defining what I wanted for myself. Having locks inspires me to be myself, to show and share what that means.

"I have chosen to put myself in the face of judgment," Noah continued. "It has allowed me to not be afraid of challenging the norm, to accept and not be affected by the ridicule or judgment or prejudice everyone has. You have to have thick skin—that's audacity."

Our dreams are always there, hidden deep within us. We just have to develop the courage and the audacity to do what it takes to achieve them despite what others may think of us. Media mogul Alexandra Cameron says it best: "Audacity is behaving as you re-ally are. I just try to be me, and I am unapologetic about it."

BE BOLD. TAKE RISKS.

"Audacity had a big impact on our success," custom vehicle creator Marc Parker told me. "If you look up audacity in the dictionary, it means boldness . . . being a trendsetter instead of a follower and having the confidence within yourself to do the things that every-one says can't be done. You have to be bold if you're going to change the game. You've got to take risks. You've got to be confi-dent in your abilities. Because you can't do it halfway. You either do it all the way, or you don't do it at all."

Almost by definition, being a Game Changer requires audac-ity. It's as if boldness and risk taking are part of the Game Changer DNA. That was definitely the case for Rene Anselmo, the founder of PanAmSat (the company I went to work for after college) and one of my mentors. In the 1960s, he launched the first Spanish network in the United States—Spanish International Network. Rene could have easily retired when he sold SIN in the 1980s for $80 million. Instead, at age sixty-one, he had the audacity to launch the world's first privately owned global satellite system. Funding PanAmSat with his own money, he attacked the monopoly on satellite transmission held by Intelsat, which was owned at the time by 120 world governments, including the United States. Critics called it a "foolhardy venture," but Rene bought a satellite and then launched it, uninsured, on the maiden flight of the Ariane 4 rocket.

Game Changers such as Rene Anselmo are like islands, standing alone in a sea of nonbelievers. Consider Martin Luther King Jr. One man speaking out in Memphis opened the aperture for people to think—maybe, just maybe, the things we believe about one another are not true. Of course, after Game Changers have proved themselves successful, their groundbreaking ideas often seem obvious. But in the early stages, they must be bold and daring in the face of sometimes overwhelming opposition.

Many years ago, I discovered that my last name, Spio, can be traced back to one of ancient Rome's greatest generals, Publius Cornelius Scipio Africanus. If ever there was an audacious Game Changer, it was Scipio. At just seventeen, he led a battle charge to save his father's life and soon thereafter stopped a plot by a large group of soldiers to desert the Roman army. Several years later, he was elected to civil office despite being under the legal age. The story goes that when the tribunes objected to his election, he replied, "If all the Roman people want to make me aedile, I am old enough."

Some years later, as the Carthaginians swept through Spain

toward Italy, Scipio's father was killed in battle. When no senior generals would lead Rome's armies into battle against the Carthaginians, Scipio offered himself as a candidate. In a precedent-setting move, the Roman people granted him a command in Spain, the first time a nonmilitary official was given a military command outside of Italy. Scipio's goal was not just to win the battle, but to turn the tide of the entire war in Rome's favor. This was an outrageous goal at the time, but Scipio had supreme confidence in his abilities.

Eight years later, Scipio defeated the great Carthaginian leader Hannibal in the Battle of Zama in Africa (202 BC), ending the Second Punic War and altering the course of history. (In honor of his victory, Scipio was given the surname Africanus.) If Hannibal had conquered Rome, the world as we know it today would be very different. Extreme audacity is not only refusing to accept defeat, but also proclaiming that you will win the war. When others say something is impossible, audacity says, "Let's go do it!"

TAKE MORE MOON SHOTS

I recently had the opportunity to spend time at Google's headquarters in Mountain View, California. It was an amazing experience in so many ways, but especially so because I was able to experience firsthand their extreme audacity. One of the most innovative, powerful and successful companies on the planet, Google's corporate strategy has been described as one part "mainstream" and one part "moon shots." Moon shots are what co-founder Larry Page calls Google's radically audacious ventures.

While most companies are focused on improving a product or service by 10 percent, Page pushes his employees to find "10X innovations"—products and services that are ten times better or more innovative than what currently exists. The moon shot mentality is evident in all of Google's game-changing developments. Who would have imagined that a search engine company would create one of the most successful mobile phone operating systems in Android? Or that an email provider would be working on a death-defying project? (Pun intended: Among Google's most daring projects is Calico, a company focused on fighting aging and extending the human life span.) Pinterest founder Ben Silbermann, who once worked at Google, said in an interview with *Inc.*, "They really had this audacity to think on a huge scale. Google was the only company that was like, we're making so much money, let's take a picture of every street in the world. Nobody does that."

Google X is the company's research and development division, run by Google cofounder Sergey Brin and scientist and entrepreneur Astro Teller, whose title is actually "captain of moon shots." Google X's mission is to identify and implement sci-fi-type products like a self-driving car, Internet access to remote areas via high-altitude balloons and their wearable computing system, Google Glass. Teller explained to *Time* magazine that rather than focusing on moneymaking ventures, Google X's projects must have three things in common: a significant problem for the world that needs solving (for example, compassion), a potential solution and the possibility of breakthrough technology. "If you make something a little bit better, people might pay you for it; they may not," he said. "But if you make the world a radically better place, the money is going to come find you, in a fair and elegant way." Google is an audacious, compassionate,

What moon shots will you take?

game-changing company and proof that when you focus on solving people's problems, uncommon success will follow.

Larry Page and Google are quintessential Game Changers—extremely audacious, ready and willing to push the envelope of, well, everything. Page says, "If you're not doing some things that are crazy, then you're doing the wrong things." Game Changers must shoot for the moon—challenge what's possible, think big and aim for 10X breakthroughs. Here are audacious world problems that need bold solutions:

- Removing space junk

- Curing devastating diseases

- Providing clean water for everyone on the planet

- Eliminating pollution

Each of us can take a page from Larry Page's playbook. Rather than asking why something hasn't been done, we should be saying, "If not me, then who will do it?" What moon shots will you take?

AUDACITY IN THE FLESH

In the course of writing this book, I interviewed many amazing people. Sandra Savage is one of those people. Sandra grew up on a beautiful farm in Kentucky. A child full of imagination, she loved music and was in the gifted program at school. Yet despite all her promise and potential, her childhood was riddled with a sense of abandonment. "I grew up feeling isolated and spent a large amount of time by myself," Sandra shared. "At the age of ten, I found some pornography magazines that sparked an addiction that began to rule my life even at that early age. Everyone looked so glamorous. I thought that was what a woman was supposed to be. The men in the magazines seemed to really like these women, and I wanted to be liked by someone. In truth, all I ever wanted was to be loved."

By the time she went to college, her addiction was full-blown. She dropped out after her sophomore year and became a go-go dancer. Sandra explained what happened next. "I first got into the sex industry when my ex-husband suggested it to bring in more income for us. I started dancing [as a stripper], thinking it wouldn't be much different than go-go dancing because I only had to take off more clothes. I said I would only work a few months, believing the lie I told myself that I could get out at any time. Those few months turned into thirteen years."

By age twenty-four, Sandra had been married and divorced twice and was addicted to alcohol, cocaine and pornography. "I was a stripper nationally and internationally and occasionally prostituted. Then I started pulling in other women to do what I had done. I became a leader in helping people step into broken-ness. It still shocks me sometimes when I remember. It seems like a different life and a different person."

By the end of her career, she was contemplating buying a brothel and launching a pornography production company. "I was at a porn convention in Miami when I found myself sitting by the pool with my suitcase, crying and trying to figure out how to change my life. Surrounded by people yet completely alone, I couldn't believe how much I did not like the life I was living."

Sandra gave up her adult entertainment booking business and moved back to Kentucky. Not long after, a friend invited her to church. "I thought that was the craziest idea I had ever heard," she said. "After everything I had done and the person I had become, I didn't want to go. I felt disqualified from loving or being loved."

Eventually, Sandra saw the opportunity to use her history as her ministry. Having been in the industry, she understood the challenges sex industry workers face. She began by launching a recovery program for women who struggle with pornography and relationship addiction. A few years later, she founded the non-profit organization BeLoved Ministries Inc. to set up systems to care for people affected by the sex industry, whether they are adult entertainers, managers, prostitutes, club owners or housewives addicted to porn.

"BeLoved teams go into strip clubs, and we give gifts with our contact info on them. We also let the workers know that they are loved and that we are here to support them. My passion is for everyone to know they are loved, no matter who they are or what they have done or are doing."

Sandra has been clean and sober since 1996. She and her husband, whom she calls the man of her dreams, have started churches and outreach programs around the country in nightclubs, cafés and tattoo parlors—all with the purpose of caring for those in the sex trade. I asked Sandra if she gets "pushback" for ministering to the sex industry. "We tend to not get pushback from the industry but rather from religious folk," she said.

When I asked Sandra if she sees herself as a Game Changer, she said, "Yes—and I believe everyone can be a Game Changer if they choose to be. It just takes one risky step—going out and doing the thing they are passionate about. It takes courage to do what's necessary despite public opinion or reputation and to do what your heart leads you to do. It may fail, but if you don't try you will never know if it could have succeeded."

Not only did Sandra dramatically turn her own life around, she is passionately committed to helping others in the sex industry do the same, combating the cycle of abuse by helping women find their value. Bold, courageous and audacious, Sandra Savage is a true Game Changer.

GET AUDACIOUS

- **RECOGNIZE THAT FEAR IS A CONSTANT.** After speaking at massive events, I always have people come up to me and ask, "How are you so comfortable and fearless onstage?" The truth is that fear is a constant; I have learned to act in spite of my fear. Working with various megastars, I found it reassuring to discover that many of them are also nervous each time they go onstage. It is a conscious effort to decide to not let fear stop you, and to move forward in spite of it.

- **TAKE APPROPRIATE RISKS.** Game Changers are calculated risk takers. They walk paths that are unknown to others, but that they have prepared for. Jumping off a cliff without a parachute is reckless, not courageous.

- **MOVE FROM VIRTUAL REALITY TO ACTUAL REALITY.** A great way to strengthen your audacity muscle is by experiencing your fears virtually, by doing things you've always wanted to do but were afraid to do. By seeking new experiences outside of your comfort zone, you'll discover that they are not as bad as you imagined them to be. My company creates virtual reality experiences, and one of the requests we get a lot is from mental health professionals looking to treat phobias such as fear of flying, claustrophobia, social phobias, arachnophobia and more. By experiencing a realistic computer-generated version of what they fear, their patients gain the courage to take on those fears in real life.

- GET OUT OF YOUR COMFORT ZONE. Change your routines and habits. Travel to new places and experience different cultures. Tune your radio to a new station and listen to a different genre of music. If you worship in a certain type of place, go listen to other people worship. Trying new things gives you the courage to try even more. We tend to fear the unknown. The practice of shining a light on what we fear through knowledge leads to making our comfort zone wider and wider.

EXERCISE YOUR AUDACITY MUSCLE

Game Changers aren't necessarily born audacious. They become audacious by virtue of their experiences and environmental reinforcements. Audacity can be cultivated. With practice, one can become consistently audacious, always ready and willing to take bold action. We can grow our "audacity muscle" by taking risks and feeding our successes.

It starts with taking on small challenges. As we act with courage despite our fear, we gain confidence. We learn to trust our instincts and response abilities. We develop more confidence with each act of courage, no matter how small—speaking up at an event, talking to a stranger or just stepping out of our comfort zone. As our confidence grows, so does our boldness. Little victories give us the confidence to do more, to take bigger risks, to conquer bigger fears. The more we conquer, the more emboldened we become, stepping further and further out of our possibility zone. Little victories lead to bigger victories, and each success deposits confidence chunks, making us more and more audacious.

Many of the Game Changers I've spoken with and observed exercised their audacity muscle with practice, becoming more emboldened with each success. Starting OWN was audacious even for Oprah Winfrey, but she believed it was possible to dream that big because of the amazing successes she had already achieved. Even the TV and movie franchise *Jackass* started with small stunts that just kept growing in riskiness and scale.

Former IndyCar and current NASCAR driver Danica Patrick is the most successful woman in the history of race car driving. She likely always had audacious dreams, but she didn't wake up one day and decide to go drive NASCAR. She began her career in go-kart racing at age ten in Wisconsin. Then, as a teenager, she took the next step and moved to England to race in several Formula series. With bigger races and bigger wins under her belt, she eventually decided it was time to race with the big boys.

In 2002, Danica joined IndyCar and had a series of ever-greater accomplishments. She was the first woman to ever lead the Indianapolis 500, and her fourth-place finish still stands as the highest ever for a female driver in that race. She was named the 2005 Indy Racing League Rookie of the Year and Female Athlete of the Year in 2006. She made history in 2008 when she became the first woman to win an IndyCar race. Those successes gave her the confidence to move to NASCAR, where in 2013, she became the first female to win a NASCAR Sprint Cup Series pole. Throughout her career, Danica has used small victories to fuel bigger victories.

That which we feed grows. Courage and boldness, well fed,

become audacity. With each success and each victory over fear, our audacity grows. You can grow your audacity muscle by doing things you've always wanted to do but were afraid to do. Consistently seek new experiences that are outside of your comfort zone. The confidence you gain will strengthen your audacity muscle even more. Each success, each victory, each risk taken and conquered will embolden you. Until one day, you will do something so bold, so audacious that you will have changed the game forever.

Pit Bull Tenacity

In order to achieve greatness, you will experience failure. It's the bitter ingredient in the recipe for success. Without trying and failing, you never get the opportunity to stand in the face of your disappointments, your insecurities or your arrogance, your pride, and say "I'm stronger."

- SANYA RICHARDS-ROSS -

Every day, millions of people tuck away their dreams, hopes and desires, pretending they don't exist, while the greatness that lies within them begs and pleads, "Please don't kill me." Over the years, the desperate voice of their greatness grows softer and softer, only returning as a scream of regret in the quiet moments of their last days.

Why do we let go of our most sacred hopes, dreams and passions? Why do we walk away from that which we most want and the amazing potential that lies within us?

I believe the problem is, in part, what I call the "airbrushing of our psyche." In a world of Photoshop, computer-generated imagery, social media and literally millions of websites and television channels that constantly demand content, reality has become skewed . . . rewritten . . . altered. We have come to believe that the so-called success we see on television, Facebook and YouTube is what we should be striving for. The journey to success has become glamorized, idealized and romanticized.

The truth is that the journey to greatness is not always pretty. It's marred with imperfections, bumps and bruises. But that reality has been airbrushed away. As a result, we use unrealistic criteria to define our own success and a flawed measuring stick to gauge our progress toward it. It is similar to young girls looking at airbrushed photos of glamorous models and celebrities and believing that is the standard of beauty they must achieve for themselves. Yet it is an unattainable standard because it isn't real.

Likewise, perfectly awesome people look at themselves and their dreams and think they aren't good enough because they compare themselves to false standards of success. They believe they and their dreams aren't worthy because they don't have thousands of "followers" or "likes." They assume they are doing something wrong when they encounter challenges or if they don't make a million dollars within the first few years of pursuing that dream.

Achieving uncommon success is neither easy nor quick. If it were, everyone would be living their full potential, and sadly, that isn't the case. The journey to greatness is filled with challenges, failure, rejection, criticism, setbacks, doubt, fear and an incredible amount of hard work. The measure of our greatness is often found not in our accomplishments, but in what each of us chooses to do when we face these obstacles. What do we do in those terrifying, nausea-inducing moments when we find ourselves dangling at the end of our proverbial rope, holding on with white-tipped fingers of a single, slipping hand? Do we hold on—fighting, kicking and clawing our way back up, inch by inch? Or do we give up, let go of the rope and fall to a life of dull regret?

Achieving greatness and game-changing success requires grabbing on to the rope of your dreams and refusing to let go, like a dog grabs on to a rope toy with its teeth and can't be shaken off.

Have you ever seen a picture of a dog dangling in midair, holding on to a rope by its teeth? That is the picture of what I call "pit bull tenacity"—unshakeable commitment, clinging to your dream with every last bit of strength you have.

Tenacity comes from the Latin word *tenere*, which means "to hold on to." Game Changers hold on to their vision at all costs—relying on faith to get them through the valley of the shadow of doubt, confronting challenges head-on, always moving forward toward their goal, patiently waiting for the fruits of their efforts and learning from their failures. If you desire to make a major change and unleash the greatness within you, you must hold on to your vision with pit bull tenacity no matter what life throws your way.

FIRST, HAVE FAITH

Many people do not achieve what they are capable of because deep down they do not fully believe in their capabilities or their dream. So when times get tough, they simply give up. If you do not have 100 percent conviction in your vision, you will turn back when the waves get big and scary. You will start doubting yourself and second-guessing your vision. You will convince yourself of all the reasons to give up rather than looking for ways to fight through it.

A good deal of tenacity is about mind-set and beliefs. The will does what the mind sees. Game Changers persist in the face of difficulty and great challenges because they have faith in the outcome. They steadfastly believe in their vision and their ability to make their goals a reality. As I'll share with you later in this chapter, I've lost everything and come back. Try raising a million dollars for a new venture after losing your company. People try to wipe the floor with your dignity. I'm often asked how I was able to do it. I explain that the one thing I have always been certain of is success in the end.

Tenacity is a test of faith—faith in oneself, faith in the vision, faith in the outcome. It is pressing on and still believing in the possibilities despite everything that speaks to the contrary. It's staring a lot of money in the face and walking away from the wrong deal because you know the right deal is still out there somewhere. It's facing the shame of eviction and unpaid bills because you refuse to get a day job so you can build your own business. It's having thick skin and ignoring the naysayers who don't see your vision. In the 1970s, Digital Equipment Corporation (DEC) was a major force in computing. Cofounder and DEC president

> You must have great faith in yourself and your vision

Ken Olsen said then of Bill Gates's invention of the microcomputer, "There is no reason anyone would want a computer in their home." Often even the so-called experts cannot see your vision. To be a Game Changer, you must have great faith in yourself and your vision.

When faced with what seems like an insurmountable challenge, check in with your faith. Take a few minutes to be still. Stillness is meditative; it is an opportunity to seek an answer and to listen for an answer to emerge. When you're too tired to stand on your feet, it's time to get on your knees. Prayer is not just for the religious. It is an opportunity for the mind to rest and refocus. Prayer is our deepest and most sincere expression of intent, hopes and desires, an affirmation of our belief in the possibilities.

Changing the game is a faith exercise. Be so confident of

success that you are willing go through a thousand "no's" to find your "yes." Act as if you know the results are certain. There is a tremendous sense of freedom that comes from knowing that if you persist, you will always succeed in the end . . . and you will.

EXPECT CHALLENGES

Not long ago, I received an email from a woman who thinks her family is under a dark cloud. Whenever she encounters a setback, she believes it's because it is her fate to fail. Such thinking assumes that challenges are personal and thus unfair, and that others have been dealt a better hand. Of course, this isn't true. Everyone will be tested in some way on their quest to personal greatness.

"There is nobody out there who has ever been successful that started off and walked straight to the end without having a problem," said Marc Parker of Parker Brothers Concepts. "I think especially in modern society, a lot of people give up way too easily. The difference between people that are successful and people that aren't is that when they hit those stumbling blocks, they find a way past them instead of quitting."

It is a given, as sure as the sunrise and sunset—whenever you begin anything of significance, challenges show up. It is almost as if fate is determined to test your passion, your commitment, your resolve. In fact, challenges and obstacles are a crucial part of the combination to unlocking the greatness that lies within each of us. It is in overcoming struggles that our character and our significance are molded.

Tenacious people know that difficulties are just par for the course. Telecommunications entrepreneur and Game Changer Mike Gallagher is no stranger to challenges. "Whenever you start a venture, there are invisible forces working against you in the marketplace trying to keep you out," he told me. That invisible hand of the market is constantly pushing against you. Once you get through that and get something going, those same forces start working for you. Carving out your own space in any endeavor is extremely difficult. You have to be tenacious."

I can't begin to tell you the challenges that I've faced on my journey. I've learned to expect the "noise." But I view every challenge as an investment in the future. When challenges appear, I suck it up and push through, knowing that once the tide turns and the forces pushing against me start to work for me, they will propel me forward.

Challenges and setbacks can also be signposts alerting you that you need to change course or adjust your strategy. I love the Rascal Flatts song "Bless the Broken Road." Part of the lyrics state: "Every long-lost dream led me to where you are." Setbacks can be like North Stars guiding us to our true north. For example, perhaps you applied for your dream job or to your dream school, but you didn't get the job or the school didn't accept you. That doesn't mean your dream is wrong and you should give up on it. It means that particular job or school wouldn't take you down the right path. It means there exists another situation that, although you can't see it now, will eventually lead you to your ultimate goal. People often say, in retrospect, that losing their job was the best thing that ever happened to them because it forced them out of a comfortable place and into their true passion.

The "no's" of life often point you in the direction of your ultimate "yes." There's an old saying that not getting what you want could be the best stroke of luck. Both Justin Timberlake and Britney Spears lost on the 1980s TV show *Star Search*. If they had won, they never would have auditioned for *The Mickey Mouse Club*, which set the course of their respective futures. When a situation isn't working out as you had expected or hoped, look at it as an opportunity to rename your battle. Instead of seeing it as a failure, see it as your North Star pointing you toward something better.

In an interview on E! Television's *Pop Innovators*, Black Eyed Peas founding member will.i.am said, "Most people think 'no' [means] no. I think 'no' [means] 'to know'—to know the parameters, to know what's possible. And then with that knowledge, you can do anything that you put your mind to." If you embrace that perspective in life, then when you get a "no," you come away thinking, "What do I need to know? Is there something I need to do better to communicate what I'm doing or to find the right audience for my cause? How can I sharpen the focus?" At some point in your journey, people are going to turn you down and turn you away. Learn as much as you can from your "no's" so that you can get to your "yes" that much more quickly.

Alex Cameron is a woman who completely changed the game in the hip-hop industry. "If someone insults you or says they don't like an idea, you can't walk away with your tail between your legs," she told me. "You have to keep pushing. You have to look for the next opportunity. You have to believe in yourself. How much are you willing to struggle through? How many no's are you willing to take? How thick skinned are you? Ultimately, your level of success has a lot to do with how much grit you have."

Every Game Changer has had moments of challenge and circumstances that they've had to overcome. They are committed to finding a way around, over, under or through any obstacle they might encounter. In many ways, tenacity is the ultimate exercise in creativity. It is tasking the mind, soul and body to search for a suitable solution to a challenge or obstacle that stands in our way. Game Changer Noah Graj had this to say about tenacity: "I don't accept when someone says something is impossible. When somebody says something isn't possible, what they are really saying is that we haven't been creative enough to find the solution, to find a way to make it happen. I am tenacious in that I don't accept what other people say is true and instead create what I believe to be true."

When you set out on your journey to greatness, know from the outset that you will undoubtedly encounter obstacles and challenges. When you come upon a roadblock, stop, take a breather, assess the situation and decide if you need to change direction. If the path forward is the correct one, push onward. Persevere. And don't take challenges personally. The universe is not working against you . . . it's preparing you for the greatness ahead.

KEEP MOVING

Not long ago I traveled to China on a seven-city tour on behalf of the U.S. Department of State. On the fifteen-hour flight, I sat next to a Chinese man who told me a wonderful story.

A woman suffering from an illness heard of a doctor with a great track record of healing this particular ailment. But the doctor lived in the faraway village of Makalu. At the time, there were no roads leading into the village, so the woman had to make the long journey on foot. After walking for days, she came upon a sign on the trail that indicated Makalu was still eighty kilometers away.

Completely defeated, she decided to give up and return home. As she sat, gathering her strength for the return trip, she saw a man walking toward her. Thirsty, she asked him for water. The man said he had none, but told her there was a family that lived on the edge of Makalu and often welcomed visitors with water. "Sir, I simply do not have the strength to get to the village. My legs will not carry me another eighty kilometers to Makalu," the woman replied as she pointed to the handwritten sign. Smiling, the man said, "Woman, you are five minutes from Makalu. The children of the village like to prank travelers by replacing the welcome sign with this sign."

So often, we don't know how close we are to our goal and give up. Unlike a race, there is often no clearly marked finish line on the road to greatness. Too many people quit on themselves and their dreams, not realizing the success they seek is just a few steps away. Game Changers never stop moving toward their goal. They know that if they work relentlessly success is guaranteed, but they never know when they will find it. They could achieve their dream tomorrow, or it could be years down the road. Game Changers know that the secret to winning is persistent action—the best way to position themselves for a win is to just keep moving, putting one foot in front of the other.

> The secret to winning is persistent action.

What is the next step you need to take toward your dream? Set some milestone goals and get going. Don't be distracted by people who try to discourage you, like the children of the village in the story above. Celebrate the milestones when you achieve them. Those little victories will offer proof of your progress and give you the energy to keep going. Success may be miles down the road . . .

but it could be just around the corner. Either way, you will cross that finish line if you just don't stop.

DON'T UPROOT YOUR DREAM
BEFORE IT HAS A CHANCE TO GROW

One of the outcomes of the airbrushing of our collective psyche is that we have become an instant-gratification society. We want immediate results. We want to believe the stories we hear of instant wealth and overnight success. But there is no such thing as overnight success. What we don't know about those who are dubbed overnight successes is the years of behind-the-scenes hard work they put in. Truth be told, true success takes time.

Winning big in the lottery is the closest one can get to overnight success. But there is no way to duplicate that result other than buying a lottery ticket, and with the odds of winning millions to one, that doesn't seem like a very good strategy. However, let's suppose for a moment that you did have a winning lottery ticket worth $1 million, but the lottery office said you couldn't pick up your winnings for a year. Would you rip up the ticket and throw it away because you had to wait for your prize? Or would you be patient and start making thoughtful plans for your winnings? How long would you be willing to wait for the prize of a lifetime? One year? Three years? Five years?

Most people would wait as long as five years for $1 million. Yet ironically they won't give their hopes, dreams and aspirations the same time. All too often, great dreams are smashed on the rocks of impatience. When we plant a seed, we don't keep uprooting it to see if it's growing. We know we must nurture it, be patient and give it time to grow. Yet many of us are not patient with our dreams. If we don't see results fast enough, we panic, wondering if and when it will come to fruition. Without patience, we stop nurturing our dream, and it quickly dies before it ever has a chance to take root.

Achieving uncommon success is a process that requires patience, and Game Changers are committed to seeing the process through. They understand that patience is not only a virtue, but also a key part of tenacity. Mike Gallagher founded his game-changing company Florida Digital Network in the late 1990s. Initially the company took off, but within a few years, times got tough. "We definitely had setbacks," Mike explained in our interview. "The entire market collapsed in 2001, so financing dried up. The enterprise needed constant financing, either debt or equity. We had to eat rock soup for two years while we waited for the industry to come back. We had to really tighten down to survive."

How many people would have held on to their vision for two years? How long would you be willing to wait to attain your dreams and goals? If you achieved them on the very last day of your life, wouldn't that be better than never achieving them at all? There is no timeline for achieving one's dreams. It's a fight to live one's truth, and if it takes a lifetime, so be it.

Nothing of value starts at maturity. Patiently nurture your vision until it grows to fruition. It will work, if you work it. Impatience is a sign that you're not working hard enough, and the best antidote is effort. If you start to feel impatient because you're not seeing the results you'd like, increase your efforts. Step it up a notch. Do more to push past the stagnation.

Everyone has within them the seeds of greatness; it's a matter of patiently and persistently nurturing those seeds in order for them to grow into giant oaks.

START COUNTING WHEN IT STARTS HURTING

A reporter supposedly once asked Muhammad Ali about the number of sit-ups he could do. Ali reportedly said, "I don't count my sit-ups. I only start counting when it starts hurting. That is when I start counting, because then it really counts. That's what makes you a champion."

Changing the game involves some discomfort. Change happens when you push past your limits, whether they be physical, mental or emotional. Every time you reach what you think is your limit and fight through it, you strengthen your tenacity muscle and redefine your "normal" limits. When you hit a point where you want to quit, do ten more of whatever you're doing. Run ten more yards, read ten more lines, call ten more prospects or investors, work ten more minutes, come up with ten more ideas. As you stretch yourself to go further, last longer, work harder, you become more capable of reaching your dreams and goals. Ironically, when you push past the pain, your effort actually becomes easier and more enjoyable, much like the so-called runner's high.

If you're uncomfortable, be encouraged—you're on the right track. Double down! This is the time to increase your efforts. That is exactly what Waymon Armstrong did. Seeing the possibilities for computer simulation, Waymon left his job and founded Engineering & Computer Simulations (ECS) in 1997. But by 2001, ECS was struggling to stay in business. Waymon knocked on practically every door in search of opportunities for his company. Employees worked without pay. Waymon's wife, Frances, went back to work, holding down two jobs to support the family, and offered her pristine credit to secure the loans that kept the company going.

With a crushing $700,000 in credit card debt on his back, Waymon flew from Florida to California in search of a needle in a haystack—a certain military officer at a military conference. This officer was the key to a deal that could turn ECS around. Waymon states in an interview with *I4 Business* that the only information he had about the officer was his name and a photo. At the conference, Waymon was confronted with "hundreds of men in the same uniform with the same haircut." After several days of searching, he found his target and introduced himself. The bet paid off, with Waymon securing a contract that kept the business afloat and changed the course of his fate. By 2009, Waymon had repaid all of his debts in full. Today, ECS is thriving with tens of millions in revenue and changing the way people learn through virtual simulation.

The strongest steel is forged through the hottest flames. In order to achieve uncommon success, you have to get comfortable with being uncomfortable. As they say in the military, pain is weakness leaving the body. It is what you do when you're hurting that determines your success. In every moment of discomfort when you do that something extra, you are building the foundation upon which you will create your legacy.

HARNESS YOUR INNER PIT BULL

- **CONVENE YOUR INVISIBLE COUNCIL.** When I was about to give birth to my son, my mom told me, "Remember, there are billions of people on earth. That means you are not the first to do this. If it were that awful, there wouldn't be that many people." There are many others who have gone before you, no matter your endeavor. Seek them out and let their stories inspire you on your journey. I wrote this book because the Game Changers herein, along with many others, have provided me with unbound courage and the fuel to hang on no matter what is thrown my way. I have an invisible council of advisors and mentors—people whose values and principles align with mine. Their words and journeys inspire and fuel me. Assemble yours.

- TAKE THE SCIENTIFIC APPROACH TO FAILURE. Engineers love sharing spectacular failures on the way to surprising successes, because they consider each failed experiment as a tool in their toolkit, something they now know not to do. Do not personalize challenges. Wring the lessons out of each setback, and use them to do better the next time. Do not be afraid of the criticism or the shame that comes with not getting it right the first time. Many people who have given up on their dreams attempt to cause others to give up by brutally critiquing; don't join that sad club by giving up.

- ANTICIPATE AND PREPARE FOR CHALLENGES. The fight to live your truth is among the toughest things you will face. Mentally prepare for obstacles to come your way. There are times when you will be filled with doubt, anxiety, fear, even depression. Know that everyone goes through this process. It is transient. Let it pass.

- BUILD A SUPPORT STRUCTURE. This is perhaps the most important advice in this book. Your support structure will take you further than anything else. The stronger your support structure, the further you will get. One of my good

friends always says, "Thank God it's us." No matter the challenge we are facing, those are his first words, because together he knows we can get through the storm.

- **REMEMBER THAT SACRIFICE IS NOT THE SAME AS LOSS.**
  Making sacrifices today for a lifetime of living the life you
  desire is an investment and shouldn't be seen as a loss.
  Rockets are usually deployed with deadweight or ballast on
  board to help steady the flight. The ballast is lost along the
  way as the flight rises higher and higher. Think of the things
  that you have to sacrifice as ballast—deadweight that you no
  longer need as you gain the discipline to rise to your goal.

FAILURE IS A GIFTED TEACHER

If we are open and willing to learn, failure can teach us life's most
powerful lessons and help us discover our greatest assets. Everything that we experience in life—the good and the bad—is a
learning opportunity that can benefit us in the future. But failure
teaches in a way that success cannot.

Every so often life makes a decision on our behalf that we are
unwilling to make ourselves. We can choose to see it as a blessing
or a curse. We can choose to build a bridge or a wall with the
stones that life throws our way. Each time we face a setback, the
perspective we take makes a world of difference in how we pro-
ceed and if we are able to hold on. My father used to tell me,
"Name your battles correctly!" What he meant is that how we
view a situation is all in our perspective. What others called failure, I could call feedback. Instead of seeing a roadblock, I could
choose to see a turning point in the journey to success. A mistake

is really just a "missed take"—a "do-over," just like actors do another take when filming a movie. That wise advice from my father served me well during the most difficult time of my life.

In 2008, I founded Gen2Media (now Vidaroo), a technology and marketing company. As business was heating up, I was approached by a very successful investor who had a vision to take my company public. In exchange for his capital, he wanted to be the CEO and a member of the board of directors. I agreed to him taking the helm, as I had no prior experience running a publicly traded company. Also on the board were a CFO hired by the investor, a brilliant programmer I had hired, my two original partners and me.

By 2010, we were on top of the world. We had 1,300 percent revenue growth over the year before and were doing business with the likes of Microsoft Xbox and the Coca-Cola Company. We even worked on the Super Bowl halftime show featuring the Black Eyed Peas. With our star rapidly rising, the investor hatched a plan (unbeknownst to me) to take the company public without any interference from me. His idea was to make a quick buck by taking the company public as soon as possible (rather than waiting to create more value in the company and making more money in the long run), and in order to do that he had to push me out first. I later learned that the programmer I had hired was also lobbying the board behind me, trying to convince them that he should be running the company.

The very people I had brought in eventually voted me out of my own company. To add insult to injury, I had a noncompete clause, which prevented me from doing what I loved—solving problems for clients and telling their stories through technology, marketing and video production. Contemporary carnivores that these people were, they forgot that the strength of the business was based on my vision and hard-earned relationships. When I was kicked out, all but a few of the salespeople left and many of their biggest clients walked away. The company went from making millions in revenue to being on life support in three years. At one point, they asked me to come back and get the company on track. But that was little consolation for the tremendous loss I felt.

Perhaps the most painful part of this experience was the implications for my financial and personal life. I had used the earnings from my Boeing patents and the proceeds from mortgaging my house to start the company. I also took a minimal income while I built the company. Once the board pulled the rug out from under me, I landed with literally nothing to my name. While others were enriching themselves off a company I had poured my blood, sweat and life's savings into, I had no job, no home and I was six weeks pregnant.

Game Changers achieve uncommon success because they are willing to learn the lessons that failure always brings. They understand that failure is a powerful, although often painful and costly, teacher. I learned some incredibly valuable lessons from being booted out of my own company. For one, I learned to mind my business and pay close attention to the legal details. I now make certain that I clearly understand, line by line, corporate bylaws, articles of incorporation and other matters relating to corporate governance. I also ensure my company bylaws include a control block that gives me the final decision on any issues affecting corporate structure. And, of course, I have a clause that prevents me from ever being removed from the company.

I also learned to always listen to my instincts. When I was interviewing that amazing programmer, I felt there was something wrong, but I couldn't place it. I ignored my instincts and let his impressive skills dictate the decision. Now I realize that skill and knowledge can be acquired, but good character can't. Maya Angelou is quoted as saying, "When people show you who they are, believe them." Today, I'm very deliberate about the people I surround myself with. I make a conscious decision to only work with people I love, admire and respect. It's a choice that comes with sacrifices at times, but the peace of mind is rewarding.

As the saying goes, there is no such thing as failure, only feedback. The question is, are we open to receiving that feedback? If we allow it to, failure will clearly show us what we want and don't want, and what we need to change to set ourselves up for success in the future. Failure also increases our response ability—the ability to respond to challenges and setbacks. When I hit a roadblock now, my reaction is, "What's the lesson to learn here? What do I need to learn to get the heck out of this situation and never come back?" Every lesson learned offers more resources for the journey ahead.

I once approached a venture capitalist to invest in my company. He told me he didn't invest in entrepreneurs' first companies or in people coming fresh out of good jobs with no prior failures. "You're too green," he said. "Go fail with someone else's capital first. Then come back after you've been kicked around a bit." This man understood that failure builds your personal equity. Hardships are part of a very necessary process I call melting and molding. When you buck or bypass the system, the results are often tragic. That's why you often see people who get famous or rich overnight lose their minds. There is a process to self-mastery and you have to allow it the time it needs in the oven to bake.

Tribal marks are common in certain parts of Africa. A popular mark that people scar their faces with is the lion's mark—clawlike scratches that symbolize defeating the lions of life and standing tall to tell your story. Embrace the "scars" of your setbacks and failures and wear them proudly. They are your tribal mark. They represent the lessons, strength and personal equity you've gathered on your journey to greatness. They are proof positive of your tenacity and resolve to stand tall in the face of adversity.

Failure, challenges and setbacks are simply mileposts on the journey to greatness. Hang on to your vision with pit bull tenacity and never stop moving toward your goal, because you never know when the floodgates will open.

———————

You need thick skin. There are going to be people who won't see the wisdom of your path and your decisions, and they may try to hinder and deter your success. You need to continue on and encourage yourself to continue. You need to be your own best supporter and best cheerleader.

—LESLIE HIELEMA, INTERNATIONAL CONSULTANT
TO ENTREPRENEURS, FIRST WOMAN
PRESIDENT OF THE FIVE-STAR
ORLANDO CHAMBER OF COMMERCE

PART TWO

Break Through to Uncommon Success

In Part One, we identified the fundamental traits of people who have changed the game in one way or another. If you haven't already, take a moment to think about which of the seven traits you naturally possess. Which ones might you want to develop more? Cultivating these traits represents the first part of the formula for achieving uncommon success.

The second part of the formula is to consistently live in the center of your greatness. That means discovering your highest and best use and offering it to the world. It also involves embracing your uniqueness and living your life by design rather than by default. If you truly desire to achieve your dreams, you must start your journey here and now, no matter your situation or circumstances. And finally, you have to find your tribe—the people you are here to serve, as well as the people who are here to support you.

Anyone can follow this formula and become a Game Changer. In Part Two, I will show you how to do just that and become a "category of one." Game Changers are in a class all their own. There is no comparison or competition. There is only one Oprah, only one Steve Jobs, only one Pablo Picasso, only one Martin Luther King Jr. . . . and only one you!

Discover Your Greatness

A musician must make music, an artist must paint, a poet must write if he is to be ultimately at peace with himself. What one can be, one must be.

- ABRAHAM MASLOW -

Why am I here?

That is perhaps the most important question in life. From a very young age, we start the search for our raison d'être (French for "reason for existence"). The search for the answer is the search for significance—assurance that our being here on this planet means something. When we discover the answer to this question, it validates our existence and our lives. Finding the answer brings joy, peace and fulfillment, as well as material success.

Until this question is answered, however, we often feel as if a part of us is missing. We are restless, aimless, with a deep longing within our soul. A person without a reason for living is a danger to him/herself and the world at large. All crimes committed against self or others are expressions of a lack of purpose. Without a life of meaning and significance, the human experience becomes a breeding ground for hopelessness, and we look to unsuitable substitutes like sex, alcohol, drugs and even violence to fill the void.

Each day we hear of people who have drifted into chaos because they don't have an answer to that ultimate "why" question.

Humans have been asking the "why" question for thousands of years. I believe the answer is quite simple: We are here to discover and live our greatness. I know at my core that there is greatness in every person on the planet. Humans are designed to be champions. We are wired for challenge, not monotony. We are meant for something far greater than working a meaningless job, eating, sleeping and watching TV. That's why boredom sets in so easily for so many.

It is this yearning for greatness that compels us to admire those who have connected with their raison d'être and become seemingly more than ordinary. "Celebrity worship" is no longer limited to movie stars, rock stars or athletes; it extends to people in technology, medicine, business and even faith. We are drawn to those who challenge themselves beyond what we deem possible and achieve uncommon success. Their accomplishments speak to the champion that lies within us.

> Humans are designed to be champions.

How deeply our greatness is buried depends on how comfortable we have become with mediocrity. The question is, how committed are we to finding the treasure buried within us? If you knew a financial treasure was buried in your own backyard, you would be digging up your yard tonight with the biggest backhoe you could find, right? Are you willing to give the same effort to finding your personal treasure? Discovering your greatest use is the most important human endeavor because it determines how you will spend your time here on earth. Living your greatness is also the one thing that you must do in this life—the one battle you must win no matter what—because therein lies not only the reason for your existence, but also true happiness.

The journey to greatness starts with looking inside ourselves. I define greatness as the intersection of passion, purpose and potential. It is that place where you are radically passionate about what you're doing, you are naturally gifted to do that thing, and you are using that passion and those gifts to solve problems and serve others. Living in the center of your point of greatness allows your best and highest possible contribution to our world. When you operate in that space, you've found what you're here to do—your raison d'être.

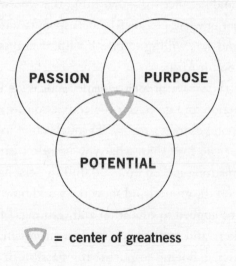

= center of greatness

Ultimately, being a Game Changer is about the pursuit of one's point of greatest contribution. When we take the time to audit and inventory the treasures we already possess, we discover that we have the ability to solve problems and change the game in a big way. Finding and living in the center of your greatness will enable you to answer the "why" question and to live a life of significant success.

LIVE YOUR PASSION

In Part One, we talked about radical passion and its importance to game-changing success. Finding your greatness—your highest point of contribution—starts with living your passion. Your passion is your calling, your personal cause, that thing you have a compulsion to do. The word "passion" comes from the Latin verb *patī*, meaning "to suffer." Your passion is that which you are willing to suffer and sacrifice for—that thing that you will stand and defend, no matter what. Nelson Mandela spent twenty-seven years in prison—and was willing to give his life if necessary—to end apartheid in South Africa.

Passion is the source of focus, hustle, audacity and tenacity. It forces bold action and gives you the conviction to keep pushing until your vision becomes a reality. It's much easier to hang on and fight for what you love than what you couldn't care less about. Waymon Armstrong racked up $700,000 in personal debt to get his company off the ground and show the world how virtual simulation could be applied to education and training. I faced ridicule from coworkers and peers when I left a promising career as a rocket scientist at Boeing to pursue my passion of publishing a magazine for singles.

I've had people tell me they have no passion or don't know how to find their passion. Like your shadow, your passion is always there in the background, following you. Your passion calls to you constantly; sometimes it whispers, and sometimes it screams. Passion is the call to be an adman whispering to engineering student Sherman Wright during a movie. Passion is the plight of the world's poor, shouting at Jessica Jackley so loudly that she answered the call by quitting her job and moving to Africa.

Passion is that thing that tugs on your soul, even when you don't know why. Often it has been with you since you were a child. Mike Gallagher was so fascinated by his neighbor's phone truck as a kid that he used to sit in it and play for hours. As a young girl, I was constantly taking things apart trying to learn how they worked. I pulled apart our radio and little television, consumed with figuring out where the information was coming from. It filled me with so much energy and excitement, I couldn't wait to get up the next morning and do it all over again.

Although you may not hear it calling, your passion is there. Here are some clues to discovering it:

- **What do you love to do?** What is that thing that you can't wait to do again and that you can see yourself doing nonstop? What energizes and enlivens you? What topics do you get completely engrossed in? What are you compelled to talk, think and learn about?

- **What do you desire, hope for, dream of?** Your passion can be found in a moment of inspiration or insight. Where does your mind wander when you daydream? Your life's passion bleeds into your unguided thoughts. What would you be doing if anything were possible? (Anything *is* possible!)

- **What situations or circumstances make you outraged or sad?** What issues do you care about deeply and desperately want to change? Passion can come from the need to escape pain. A hungry stomach, empty pocket or broken spirit can drive one to amazing heights.

- **What are you willing to fight for?** What are you fanatical about—your personal cause or revolution? What are you willing to sacrifice and work hard for every single day?

- **What is your history?** Look to your past for passion sparks. What moments stick out the most? When did you have a significant impact or make a difference for someone? When were you the happiest, the most fulfilled?

When you find your passion, you will know it. The barometer for passion is how you feel when you are engaged in the act. We are happiest when operating at the center of our passion. It has a unique feel, which is impossible to mask. When you experience it, you immediately recognize it. It feels comfortable, like an old friend . . . like "home."

MAXIMIZE YOUR POTENTIAL

Within every human being are gifts, talents and skills that are uniquely native to him or her alone. These are the things that you do naturally, that you have an unexplained knack for and that you intuitively gravitate toward. These are the things that you instinctively know and don't even know how or why you know them. The distinctive combination of your gifts, skills, talents, knowledge, insights and experiences is exactly what makes you who you are. It is also one of the three keys to your greatness and precisely what uniquely qualifies you for your purpose.

Our natural propensities, like our passions, are typically evident from an early age. My three-year-old son recently switched schools because we moved. At his previous school, his teachers jokingly referred to him as the "HOD"—head of department—because he loves to lead. To my surprise, at his new school, the teachers call him "Mayor" for the same reason. This is not something that I or anyone taught him. He naturally has the potential for leadership. Perhaps one day he will be president!

In doing research for this book, I had the incredible opportunity to interview Vernon Winfrey, Oprah's father. He shared with me that Oprah has always had an amazing talent for speaking and connecting with an audience. "You've never seen the real Oprah until you hear her speak, see her get up and address an audience," he said. "She gave a reading in church to about two hundred fifty people when she was nine years old. She gave the speech 'Invictus.' And she didn't just get up there and say, 'Blah, blah, blah.' She did it with conviction. I've never seen anything like it. People were saying, 'Brother Winfrey, that girl is going places!'" Our gifts, when combined with our passion and purpose, fuel our greatness.

Sometimes people ask me, "What if I have no gifts?" That's not possible. Everyone has some skill, talent or ability that flows naturally from them without stress. Here are some questions to help you identify your potential:

- What comes to you naturally? What is your "sweet spot"?

- What do you love about yourself?

- When and where do you do your best work, as if you are "in the zone"?

- What do people compliment you about or admire and depend on you for?

- What unique and invaluable marketable skill do you bring to the table?

When you take inventory of your gifts and talents, you will discover the seeds of your greatness. (You will also find that you are far more capable than you give yourself credit for.) These natural gifts are your tool set for the journey of life. These are the areas in which you cannot help but excel when you apply hard work and dedication. Naturally gifted athletes, with coaching and training, become world champions. Your potential is the currency for attaining what you want in life, so invest in it. When you tune in to your talents, you will start to notice opportunities to use and develop them.

All gifts, talents and skills are merely potential—that is why I say they are the *seeds* of your greatness. Talent is relative to its value or its ability to impact others. The real magic happens when you use your gifts to fuel your passion and purpose. Your potential becomes kinetic when you can find a way to apply it in the service of others, and that only happens when you hustle to find a way to make it useful. That is how you turn that potential energy into a full-blown explosion.

FOLLOW YOUR PURPOSE

No matter how passionate or talented you may be, if that passion and talent don't serve a greater good, then they are meaningless. You must find that thing that your passions and talents can serve.

My father used to say, "Don't keep your light under a bushel," meaning don't keep your gifts and talents to yourself. Your purpose is the way you share your passion and potential with the world—by solving problems and serving other people.

Solving Problems

We are all being called upon today to be problem solvers. The world is full of problems that beg solutions—the environment, space junk, pollution, hunger, poverty, disease. People love to complain and discourage, but the truth is that there is not a problem on the face of the earth without a solution. What's missing is your unique perspective. Don't think you don't matter. There are issues and challenges affecting you, your community or the world that only you can solve. Do not assume someone else has or will solve them. Be the change you want to see in the world.

> Your purpose is the way you share your passion and potential with the world.

If you are bothered by something, rather than complaining about it, why not create a solution, help others and profit from it? That's exactly what Chinedu Echeruo did. In a Google for Entrepreneurs program that I am involved with, I had the chance to briefly talk with Chinedu, a Game Changer and entrepreneur who successfully founded and sold not one but two companies. Regarding his process for developing HopStop, a pedestrian navigation app that he recently sold to Apple for an estimated $1 billion, Chinedu explained: "I've always been bad with directions. When I moved to New York to join an investment bank, I was constantly getting lost. My particular way of looking at business is to find pain points you can solve, and for me, getting around the largest city in the United States was a big pain. I was like, how come no one has solved this problem?"

If you're one who thinks, "There's got to be a different way," then follow your purpose and solve the problem. As Chinedu said, "The only determiner of success is delivering something of value to others." It's all about finding others' pain points and providing relief. Start by asking these questions:

- What is your biggest point of frustration?

- What do you complain about the most?

- What angers, saddens or annoys you and what do you want to do about it?

- What do you want to change in yourself, your community, the world?

You can brainstorm by starting with your own problem or challenge. Once you land on a problem, sit with it for a while and consider it some more. You are going to dedicate a lot of time and effort to solving this problem. Are you radically passionate about it? Do you have the skills and talents to help solve the problem? If, after letting the idea marinate, you can't shake it off, then you have discovered a purpose for which you could become successful. Next, look around within your home, then in your community, then around the globe to see if this problem affects others. Chances are, if something affects you, it affects others as well. Those who share your pain will find your promise to be valuable.

Ultimately, every problem is a human problem. Anything that solves a problem for another human being is a humanitarian act and therefore an important contribution, be it finding a cure for cancer or a cure for a broken heart, building a rocket or building a bridge, planting crops or planting ideas in children's minds.

Serving Others

Your life's work is tied to a group of people who need or love what you have to offer. In order to be a Game Changer and make an impact, you must seek out those people you are meant to serve and solve their problem. Your purpose is to reconcile their pain with a promise. Without these people, you have no purpose. A game without spectators is just a practice. A show without an audience is simply a rehearsal.

Great leaders serve their people. Mandela's journey to greatness was a fight not for himself, but for the people of South Africa. The same was true of Martin Luther King Jr. and Mahatma Gandhi. Every Game Changer throughout history has fulfilled their purpose by faithfully serving a group of people. It is only by impacting others that our greatness is unleashed.

Even artists serve others by using their passion and potential to offer beauty and joy that defeats the difficulties and sadness of life. The most successful artists are the ones who find their audience. Musical artists who don't develop their gift of voice and apply it so that others can enjoy it may be very talented, but will they be considered a success in the field of music? If the only people who enjoy their music are their mothers, they're not using their greatness. Fantasia Barrino had both passion and potential but was living on food stamps and occasionally living in her car. It wasn't until she appeared on *American Idol* that she found her people and discovered her greatness.

Likewise, the Oscar-winning documentary *Searching for Sugar Man* is the story of American folksinger and songwriter Sixto Rodriguez. Hailed as perhaps the next Bob Dylan, his albums went nowhere in the United States, and he spent his life in obscurity. Unknown to Rodriguez, however, a bootlegged copy of one of his albums made it to South Africa, where it became wildly popular and inspired a generation. He had no idea that his work had found a huge audience in another part of the world.

Fortunately, in today's socially connected world, it has become easier to find those you are here to serve. Here are a few steps to take:

- **Ask some initial questions.** Who can I help? Who would benefit from my promise? What kinds of people will love what I can do?

- **Research to find others who "speak your language."** Find those who need what you have to offer. Seek out people who are talking about the same problem or issue. Search websites, blogs, social media and other groups, communities and associations. For example, a simple Google search for "global warming" comes up with associations such as the Union of Concerned Scientists. If you want to get into this career field or start your own business in this industry, contact people who have experience in the industry and ask for their insights.

- **Create a profile of your ideal "customer."** I worked with retail genius Foot Locker on a project to reach "Sneakerheads," a term for passionate sneaker aficionados. It was on this project that I first discovered the process of creating a customer persona—a fictitious character that embodies the demographic and psychographic qualities of the people who could benefit from your purpose. (There are plenty of marketing research tools, some free, that can help you build a profile.) A profile gives you incredible insight into who your potential customer is and how solving their problem impacts them, and helps you craft language to attract them to your offering.

- **Go to your industry's Mecca.** In doing your research and creating a profile, an ecosystem will emerge—a community that supports and can house your vision. Central to this ecosystem is your industry's Mecca. This is the richest soil in which to plant your seed. You must go where your people are. (Thanks to technology, you don't have to physically go there—you can find your Mecca via the web.) By going there you can vet your promise and find others who share your vision and speak your language. A life-changing trip I took to Silicon Valley created a complete shift in my thinking and connected me with a number of amazing people in Internet entrepreneurship.

- **Listen and tweak.** Listen to those whom you serve, who share your vision and who have been where you want to go. Use the feedback to improve, scale and grow your vision. As a marketing company, this is the process we use to help businesses find, grow, engage and ultimately monetize their products and services.

OFFERING YOUR BEST
AND HIGHEST CONTRIBUTION

To change the game, you must live your greatness by offering your best and highest contribution to the world. This encapsulates your life's journey. You will find your greatness at the confluence of your passion, potential and purpose. If any of the three are missing, you cannot operate within your greatness.

For example, you may be incredibly passionate about a cause and have found the people you are here to serve. Yet if you lack the requisite skills and talents to support that purpose, that problem is best left to someone else to solve. Your greatness lies elsewhere. Every day, amazing talents are lost in the world because when people operate outside their point of greatest contribution, their true talents never surface. If you stay where your weakness thrives, your strengths will wilt and possibly die. There are many problems in the world that I am passionate about but don't have the talent to solve. If I were to pursue these, my efforts would be wasted because I can't bring the right skills to bear upon them. Working your fingers to the bone gets you nothing more than carpal tunnel syndrome if you don't have a natural gift for what you're doing.

On the other hand, what if you possess the skills to solve a problem, but have no passion for it? Sadly, this is where so many people find themselves—doing passionless work. If you are in a job where you are constantly watching the clock, dreading Mondays and looking forward to retirement, then you are not connected with your greatness. You may be exceptionally good at your work, but without passion you are only feeding mediocrity. And feeding mediocrity kills your greatness. You will be only mediocre at best doing what you are not passionate about. Without

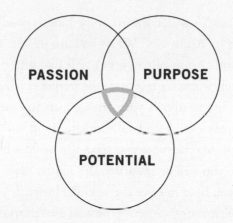

PASSION: Helping people live their dreams. Connecting and inspiring people.

POTENTIAL: Coming up with new ideas and solutions. Coaching/teaching, writing.

PURPOSE: End inequality, injustice, poverty/lack. Help people who feel lonely, isolated, lost, unfulfilled. Remove ingnorance.

 MY CENTER OF GREATNESS: Help people live their greatness by equipping them with the necessary tools.

the spark of passion, no matter how much fuel you pour on, there will be no fire.

We are not going for average or mediocre. We are going for awesomeness. We are shooting for the moon. To be a Game Changer is to live your passion, maximize your potential and follow your purpose. It takes all three. Here is how passion, potential and purpose have come together in my life:

When you find your best and highest contribution to the world, as I believe I have, you experience an all-encompassing feeling of joy, peace and satisfaction. A good friend of mine describes it as "feeling your baby leaping." In London, they would say,

"Bob's your uncle"—which means everything is good. In Jamaica, the expression is "All is *irie*." When you are in "the zone," you're simply beautiful. A fish out of water will flail and die, but in its natural element, water, its true genius emerges. Living in the center of your greatness allows your true genius to emerge, and the natural outcomes are joy and fulfillment, along with tangible rewards and fortune. The more you serve the world with your greatness, the more you will be rewarded. It's nature's law.

What do you have to offer the world? How will you choose to serve others with your passions, potential and purpose? Until you pursue it, you will never know the far-reaching impact of your greatness. Remember that you are a significant part of the world's future. This might sound dramatic, but I truly believe that the future of our world depends on each of us finding and living our greatness. Imagine that we could be missing out on solutions to our most pressing global problems because too many people believe they have nothing significant to offer. I hope you don't dismiss me when I tell you that our future depends on each and every one of us contributing our best and highest self. This is why I have made it my life's mission to help others find and set ablaze their greatness.

Your greatness will likely manifest itself in different ways throughout your life, but all will be points where your passions, potential and purpose meet. Noah Graj's greatness manifested in very different ways through his branding work with Graj + Gustavsen, through Urban Farmers and through Dream Talks. Mine was revealed through my work in satellite communications, digital cinema, video marketing and matchmaking. As humans we are infinitely dimensioned. At any point in your life, as long as you are living in that space where your passion, potential and purpose intersect, you will be able to make a huge difference and impact with your life.

YOU NEVER KNOW WHERE
THE JOURNEY WILL TAKE YOU

The journey to discovering your greatness is just that—a journey, full of twists and turns and unexpected changes in direction. And sometimes you end up in the most unlikely of places. Alexandra Cameron discovered her greatness and used it to change the game in the most unlikely of industries. I first met Alex when I went to pitch my company's (Gen2Media—now Vidaroo) software to Emmis Communications. Alex was the general manager at the time, and when she walked in the room, the respect she commanded was simply amazing.

Alex faced significant struggles early in life, including dysfunctional family dynamics, economic hardship and losing her mother when she was just sixteen years old. "My journey was somewhat unorthodox," she says. "I was a latchkey kid, left to my own devices a lot, and I had two younger sisters [to care for]. I think that was the beginning of me deciding who it was that I wanted to be, who I needed to be. I clearly remember a conscious decision in my youth of realizing that no one was going to take care of me, and I was going to have to take care of myself."

Alex began working at age fifteen, and her first career job was as a bank teller. Eventually, she landed in radio, initially interning for free to learn the business, then working her way up through various positions including writer, reporter, account executive, show cohost, news anchor and sales manager. In 2008, she was named senior vice president and general manager for Emmis

Communications and New York's iconic radio station Hot 97, considered the "mother of hip-hop."

As she gained a native understanding of the hip-hop genre and culture, Alex found many similarities with her own life—growing up poor, having to overcome challenge after challenge, and being "labeled" by others. "[Before coming to Hot 97,] I knew hip-hop music and had listened to it from time to time, but I wasn't a die-hard hip-hop fan. I have learned so much working for this brand and for the people behind the logo. There are real stories behind hip-hop music; real meaning in where hip-hop and rap came from, the artistic expression, why rap and hip-hop artists grew and why this became such a predominant lifestyle. And it's not just music—it truly is a lifestyle. At the end of the day, hip-hop is about articulating a struggle and how to conquer that struggle, and I think we can all identify and relate with that. The lyrics are not always politically correct, not polite, and I think that's what I love about it. I am amazed by some of the artists in this format, and the things they've seen, experienced or have overcome in life. They have inspired a whole generation. Whether you're into hip-hop or not, I think that is something that you've got to respect and that is very unique to this genre and lifestyle."

Despite the fact that Hot 97 was one of the most lucrative and highest-grossing radio stations in the country, Alex quickly realized that advertisers wouldn't support it. "Even with Hot 97's fame and success, there were a lot of stereotypes [about hip-hop] among advertisers, ad buyers and people who are not fans of hip-hop. But you'd be very surprised at who the audience is today and even who the audience was back then."

This lit her passion to change the way the world perceives hip-hop. She became a leader in defining the urban demographic and helping the world see hip-hop as a culture and mind-set rather than a race, a notion that Alex herself embodies. You see, Alex doesn't fit the image most people have when they hear hip-hop. "When you think of hip-hop, you don't think of a petite, blond Canadian chick," she says.

Alex worked tirelessly to debunk stereotypes, bringing the hip-hop culture and lifestyle into the mainstream and catapulting the value of the musical genre in the process. But she didn't stop there. Alex also changed the game in the radio industry by being the first to transform her radio station into a bona fide media company. Not only was she responsible for launching a television show based on Hot 97 on VH1, she also built Loud Digital Network, securing deals to produce events such as the Sundance Film Festival, the Grammy Awards and the Golden Globe Awards. With over fifty premium digital properties and sixty million unique monthly users, Loud Digital Network is one of the largest online entertainment and music networks, outranking Yahoo! Music, AOL Music and BET Network. She has since gone on to become the CEO of Keek, one of the largest social video-sharing platforms.

Alex's commitment to ensure that hip-hop receives its due respect, combined with her creativity and financial and business acumen, and her mission to serve those who are part of the hip-hop culture, have made her one of the most influential women in radio and media today. Alexandra Cameron has truly discovered her greatness—her best and highest point of contribution.

The magic that will make your soul soar lives in the center of your passion, potential and purpose. That is the resting place of the sun of greatness, the sun of significance and the sun of change. It is here that the giant of your greatness lies sleeping, comforted by the blanket of mediocrity. It's time to pull that comfortable blanket off, shake the audacious giant awake and allow it to guide your life. Your destiny is calling.

Embrace Your Difference

In order to be irreplaceable one must always be different.

- COCO CHANEL -

In the 1970s, Sylvester Stallone was a struggling actor frustrated with the direction of his career. He had earned parts in a few movies, but didn't have the looks or charm typical of the leading men of the time (such as Robert Redford, Burt Reynolds, Ryan O'Neal). So he diversified into writing. Stallone has said, "Early in my acting career I realized the only way I would ever prove myself was to create my own role in my own script." Envisioning himself as the leading man, he wrote a screenplay based on the true story of boxer Chuck Wepner, a mediocre boxer who stayed in the ring with Muhammad Ali for fifteen rounds on nothing but sheer determination.

When Stallone shopped the completed script, a number of production houses were interested. There was just one problem: They didn't want him in the lead role. Despite having only $106 in his bank account at the time, he turned down offers for hundreds of thousands of dollars. Stallone knew that he was different from other matinee-idol actors, and Rocky Balboa was a different kind of movie hero. He was only willing to sell the script to the producers who would allow him to play the lead. Talk about faith in his vision! Finally, Bob Chartoff and Irwin Winkler agreed to him playing the lead, although the studio only paid Stallone scale for his acting work.

Rather than cursing or fighting the fact that he was different from other popular actors, Sylvester Stallone embraced his uniqueness and created value for himself. He changed the game, along with how he was perceived, and catapulted himself and *Rocky* into movie history. *Rocky* became the first sports-themed movie to win an Oscar for Best Picture (1977) and launched Sylvester Stallone's long and lucrative acting career.

The single greatest currency that Game Changers possess is their difference, and the same is true for you. Your difference is the currency to secure your future. It is imperative that you not only embrace your difference, but also appreciate and recognize it as truly valuable and as the key to capturing your position at the Game Changer table. When you come to the table with a full plate rather than an appetite, everyone can share instead of compete.

> Your difference is the currency to secure your future.

THE IMPORTANCE OF DIFFERENCE

The subject of diversity has been given untold amounts of time and attention in the last several decades. And for good reason—it's a critically important subject. But why? Why is accepting and appreciating our fellow man's differences so important? Because a sustainable human experience is only possible in a diverse society that can peacefully coexist. Yet it seems that there is a human tendency to fear that which is different. Someone or something that is different from us is often seen as a threat rather than an opportunity, as something to be feared rather than explored and celebrated. Genocide, ethnic cleansing, racism and a multitude of wars are based on fearful reactions to different cultures, races, religions, beliefs or philosophies.

Yet our very presence and continued survival on this planet is founded on differences. Everything we see and experience around us is a result of diversity, from plant and animal life to every advancement in the man-made world. Without diversity, life as we know it wouldn't exist. Natural selection and evolution are possible only because of mutations that create variations (that is, differences). Diversity leads to growth and change. Sameness leads to stagnation and ultimately decay and death. Diversity is not just a nicety. It is a necessity for survival.

Diversity is also essential to innovation. To solve really big problems, you need various perspectives. Think of all the exciting industrial, informational and technological innovations that we enjoy today. They are all possible because each of us believes differently, thinks differently, experiences the world differently and dreams differently. Those differences lead to creativity and innovation. Diversity creates a derivative effect that is amplified as each of us contributes our unique perspective. If Google had viewed Internet search the same way Yahoo! or others did, it wouldn't be one of the most powerful companies in the world today. Every business that exists is a result of the founder's difference—they see a situation, product or service differently than anyone else sees it. Starting and growing a business is a pure exercise in self-mastery, believing in what you have to contribute and knowing exactly how it differs. Whether you start your own business or work for someone else's business, you need to know and embrace your unique value proposition.

Imagine a team where all the players played the same position or a business where all the employees did the same job. There would be chaos. It simply doesn't work. Diversity creates the checks and balances that stabilize our world. We need the scientist and the artist, the disciplinarian and the nurturer, the dreamer and the realist. Diversity of passion, potential and purpose is what creates an orderly society, with each person contributing their greatness. Teachers, doctors, astronauts, fast-food workers, janitors—everyone has a specific role to play in society.

Think about the human body. Every part has a specific utility or purpose, and all are necessary for your body to function as a whole. Losing a single finger, no matter which one, causes you to lose grip strength. Even the pinky toe plays a role in balance and walking. When we think or act as if another person or group of people doesn't have anything of value to contribute to society simply because they are different, it's like cutting off a piece of our own body. Each of us is a crucial part of the whole. Is there a part of your body you would be willing to cut off as worthless? How about your big toe?

Every human being on the planet has something to contribute precisely because every one of us is different. Each of us holds the solution to a problem. With seven billion people and counting, together we hold the solutions to seven billion problems! It is only when we accept and value one another's differences and encourage one another to make our highest point of contribution that our world will be whole and be healed.

EMBRACE OTHERS, EMBRACE YOURSELF

When I interviewed Game Changer Noah Graj (founder of Urban Farmer and Dream Talks), I learned something quite profound. Noah intentionally puts himself in the face of other people's judgments by wearing his hair in dreadlocks.

"It is a real meditation to constantly put yourself in the face of judgment," Noah explained. "Everyone has a preconceived notion of who you are. When I first began to speak about my recent project Dream Talks, I was challenged by the lack of confidence others had in me. What initially was seen, so I've been told, was a dreadlocked guy trying to make a website. I was challenged that people could not see past my looks and find the value in my goal to help others achieve their dreams. When I was able to talk to people more, all of a sudden their idea of who I am changed.

"It's a wonderful experience to put yourself in that place. It has allowed me to not be afraid of who I am. When I allow myself to push past the judgments and rejections of others, I begin to see that through action and integrity I can show my true self and correct their misjudgments.

"By growing locks," Noah continued, "I have learned to endure and embrace the drastic difference in the way people see me and to reflect on how I may be doing the same to others. It really allows you to recognize where you judge others and to be free from those prejudices so that you can actually see others for who they really are.

"Learning to overcome judgment helps me comprehend the priceless value of what everyone has to offer in this world. Through every interaction, we are given the opportunity to love, to learn and to grow. It is my dream that we would be freed from the limiting judgments we create for ourselves that prevent so much of life from being experienced and shared."

I learned a great lesson about judgment and acceptance on a recent business trip. During my flight, I asked the flight attendant for a Diet Coke. On the first sip, I encountered an unusual taste. I called the attendant to inform her there was something wrong with my drink. "The Coke tastes funny," I explained. She laughed and said, "There's nothing wrong with it. It's not Coke, it's Pepsi." That was the first time I had ever tasted Pepsi. It occurred to me then that when people encounter something different from what they expect or have previously experienced, they often make unfair judgments. Here I was ready to discard a perfectly good glass of Pepsi because I expected it to taste like Coke. Instead, I decided to give it a try and embrace something different.

When people make judgments about you, often it has nothing to do with you but rather their expectations, limited experience or lack of exposure. People often miscategorize what they do not understand. Don't try to be something that you're not just because someone else's palate isn't sophisticated enough to discern your value. And never devalue your uniqueness or play small to fit into someone's definition of you. The next time you feel out of place or think there's something wrong with you being different from the norm, just think, "Rock on, Pepsi! You're not a bad Coke after all!"

When we dare to prejudge, make assumptions or discriminate against others, we are essentially casting certain members of society as less valuable. But judging one another only limits our individual and collective greatness. Embracing your difference is as much about valuing others' differences as it is valuing your own. Coke doesn't have to be better than Pepsi, nor does Pepsi have to be better than Coke. They are both tasty drinks . . . just different. Exploration and acceptance of our differences allows us to access the hidden treasures within each of us. You will never be able to value and celebrate your own uniqueness if you can't value and celebrate the same in others.

YOUR DIFFERENCE IS YOUR SIGNIFICANCE

You are a one-of-a-kind combination of passions, experiences, skills, talents, gifts, values, beliefs and interests, and that makes you different than any other human on the planet. Your greatness is exclusive to you, and it uniquely qualifies you to do the work that you are here to do. You have something to offer the world that no one else can offer. There are problems that only you can solve. You have the ability to change the world around you in a way that only you can. This is why your difference creates your relevance.

Rather than seeing your difference as a disadvantage, embrace it. Rather than fight it, let it propel you. Your difference is your strength and your advantage over the competition. It is Marc and Shanon Parker's unique desire and ability to design and build cutting-edge vehicles that set them apart from everyone else. It was Alex Cameron's losing her mother at an early age, growing up impoverished and having to fend for herself that ultimately led her to find her best and highest point of contribution to the world. Her difference was the key to her significance.

When you identify and embrace your difference, you can create opportunity and value. In a left-brain or right-brain world, it has always been difficult for me to be "whole-brained." This has been a struggle my entire life. People ask me, "What are you—a techie or a creative? Left-brained or right-brained? Artist or scientist?" The answer is both! I love technology as much as I love the creative side—always looking for form within function and function within form. Throughout my life, I've sought opportunities that would allow me to express both. But for a long time, a whole-brained approach was frowned upon, especially in places where people perceived it didn't fit. Some of my engineering reports were deemed too flowery. I was once even told, "A fish and a bird can fall in love, but where shall they build their nest?" I felt I needed to make a choice between the two, and people often demanded that I make a choice.

As technology grew and started taking over all our lives, I found myself at the confluence of art and science. New innovations required the artist to think like the scientist, and the scientist to think like the artist. Suddenly, my kind wasn't just wanted, we were in high demand. What had been a point of contention in the past became my calling card. I remember clearly when the shift started to occur.

At Boeing Digital Cinema, I had helped develop the technology to deliver movies digitally. One day, I was watching the movie *Crush* with other engineers, after we had encoded it but before the director previewed it. I took one look at the screen and noticed a very thin white film over it. When my colleagues said they couldn't see the white film, I thought perhaps I needed to get my eyes checked and let it go. To my surprise, when the director walked in, he stopped in the middle of the theater and said, "The contrast ratio [of the pixels] is off."

Another time, while reviewing *Star Wars: Attack of the Clones*, I noticed in certain scenes that the foreground characters seemed so clear and crisp it looked as if they had been cut and pasted onto the scene. I realized then that I could both see what the directors saw *and* understand what the engineers knew. I could work with engineers to create solutions without requiring directors to sit through hours of torture doing signal processing (a purely engineering function). I could also talk to directors in depth about contrast ratio and work to attain a beautiful balance between art and science. And I actually enjoyed the process!

I had found my sweet spot. My whole brain was now in demand, to a point where I started my own consulting company and created an online video platform for delivering movies online. I was even approached by the producers of ABC's hit show *The Bachelor* to help cast the seventh season, leveraging both the Internet and traditional avenues. I had thought of my whole-brain personality as not fitting in anywhere, yet it was that difference that allowed me to ultimately create the magic. Being uniquely me had proved to be invaluable in an unbelievable way.

It is only when you discover and embrace your difference that you open the door to the possibility of offering the world something new that doesn't exist. Dave Feller doesn't like mustard—not on a sandwich, not on a hamburger, not in a recipe. Frustrated that there wasn't a way to search the Internet for recipes that didn't contain mustard, he decided to take matters into his own hands and developed Yummly.com. With fifteen million monthly unique visitors, Yummly has become the fastest-growing food site in the world. All because Dave embraced his difference. When you synchronize who you natu-

> It is only when you discover and embrace your difference that you open the door to the possibility of offering the world something new that doesn't exist.

rally are with opportunities to make an impact, uncommon success is almost guaranteed. The journey of life, after all, is to align who you are with what you are.

YOU ARE UNIQUELY PERFECT
FOR YOUR MISSION

One of the most challenging human endeavors is to be content with one's gifts. Most people compare themselves to others and think, "That person is so much . . . more talented, smarter, thinner, funnier (or whatever else) . . . than me." In actuality, you are perfect and genetically accurate for your specific mission and journey in life. You are not meant to walk someone else's mile, and their gifts and talents would only hinder rather than help you on your journey.

I find that a lot of people want to emulate other successful people because they haven't been exposed to the possibility of being their true selves and achieving their own greatness. They believe they are somehow lacking because they don't understand the value that makes them unique. And when they end up being mediocre, trying to fit into someone else's mold, they get frustrated and tuck their dreams away, thinking they have nothing to contribute. But no one is born a liability. Every single person has something unique to offer the world.

Trying to be someone other than who you are only devalues your greatness. Oprah Winfrey has talked about how early in her career she imitated Barbara Walters. That is, until the day she mispronounced *Canada* as *Can-A-da* on air, came out of her Barbara character and cracked herself up. It was the beginning of her learning the power of being the real Oprah. If she had continued trying to be a Barbara Walters knockoff, she couldn't have possibly accomplished what she has.

Game Changers are originals, not carbon copies or duplicates. No one ever achieved uncommon success being a counterfeit or knockoff. Why imitate when you can innovate? The world didn't need another Barbara Walters; it needed an authentic Oprah. Now the world doesn't need another Oprah or Steve Jobs or Jay-Z. The world needs its first *you*!

You must find what is authentic and true to you and live that to the best of your ability. The world needs your gifts no matter what they are. My nephew recently ran for student council vice president of his school. I asked him why he didn't run for president. He said he didn't want to be president, that his interests and talents were a better fit with the vice president role. There is a Game Changer in the making! At a young age, he has already embraced his unique value and contribution.

Self-acceptance, gratitude, recognition and appreciation of your uniqueness initiate access to your true purpose. For just a minute, think of yourself as that pinky toe on the human body that we talked about earlier. You have a very specific purpose—an important role to play with respect to balance. Yet you desperately long to be the eye that gets to see the world in all its beauty. As long as you are a toe trying to be an eye, you will always struggle. You will never find lasting success. Yet if you were to accept your uniqueness and be the best little toe you can be, you would find your greatness.

There's a story about a farmer who came across an egg while tending his sheep. Assuming it had been laid by one of his hens, he put it with the rest of the chicken eggs. When the egg hatched, out came a very awkward-looking chicken. It walked funny, not at all like the other chicks. One day while standing on top of a wall, the odd chick fell. Instinctively, it began to flap its wings, and lo and behold it flew away. It turns out that it wasn't a chicken after all. It was an eagle.

Don't clip your wings to fit someone else's idea of who you should be. Embrace your difference. Be who you were born to be and fly high.

FALL IN LOVE WITH *YOU*

John Mayer says it best: "Be friends with what you are." The game of life is the fight to be who and what you were born to be and to fall in love with that person. My story is a powerful testament to that.

I became a quiet recluse when I first came to America because of how much I was teased. It started on my first day of high school in South Carolina. I sat in the front row of my English class just as I'd done so many times back home in Ghana. I remember the teacher well, but not just for her strong Southern accent. With just a few minutes of the first class remaining, she announced that an African was among us. The students looked around for a real-life *National Geographic* experience. I honestly didn't realize she was talking about me. After all, I'd never been called "African."

"Come on now! Stand up, introduce yourself to the class and tell them what your name means," she insisted as she walked over to my desk.

Everyone stared. I was mortified. I knew they were looking for tribal marks, some proof of my ethnicity. "Good day," I said proudly, after a moment's hesitation. "I bring greetings to you all from Ghana. I am Mary Akua Spio."

My words fell like laughing gas bombs. With each syllable, the class laughed louder and louder. My manner of speech apparently amused the entire class, and my outfit didn't help matters either. In my attempt to look American, I'd worn cowboy boots and a large, shiny belt similar to the one boxers receive when they win a world championship match.

I became a piñata for the class's questions and insults. "Mary? Did you change your name at the airport?" one student yelled out.

"You speak English good for an African," another student quipped. Doesn't she mean, *You speak English well?* I thought to myself.

Hoping to restore control to the class, the teacher interrupted, "So, Mary, what are your dreams? What do you want to be in the future?"

Blinking back tears, I answered, "A rocket scientist." Once again, the class exploded into laughter.

"Oh dear! That's like saying you want to be the Easter Bunny!" Ms. Smith was now having fun with me. "You ought to study something like physical education. Besides, you gotta be real smart to be any kind of scientist!"

Soon after, the bell rang and everyone dispersed. I sat frozen for a few minutes, feeling numb, filled with disbelief. Later that day, when I met with the guidance counselor, things grew worse. Without giving me any evaluative tests, she concluded that I wasn't smart enough to take classes like physics and calculus, even though I had completed both in Ghana. I was put into basic algebra and told that my primary focus should be getting rid of my African accent. The counselor's words were the final jabs through my soul. If she was right, what could my future possibly hold? I felt hopeless. I had big dreams, but without the confidence I kept quiet. I was afraid to even speak for fear of being laughed at. My voice had been silenced.

Fast-forward seven years. I found myself trudging across the Syracuse University campus, arms and legs frozen from the icy wind and snow. It was time for my senior design review—the event every engineering major dreads. The design review panel consisted of professors and representatives from the engineering industry, and they were an intimidating bunch.

I stood in the back of the class with my fellow students, squirming impatiently as we watched the review panel approach our lab stations one by one. It reminded me of the lab inspections we had endured for semesters. Don Shaw, our lab instructor, would always stop at lab station ten, my station, look at me intently and ask, "Do you know whose lab station this is?" He would then answer his own question. "This is the lab station of Eileen Collins, the first female space shuttle commander!" Even though I had used lab station ten for more than three years, everyone still called it the Space Commander's Lab Station.

As the review panel approached lab station ten, the head of the panel asked in a booming voice, "Whose lab station is this?" I could feel my heart pounding as I made my way to the front of the classroom. I hesitated for a few seconds, biting my lip, tears not far from my eyes, and I answered their question with, "Ahem . . . mine." I glanced over at Don Shaw, wondering if he had a better answer for the review board. Smiling through tears of his own, he nodded in encouragement.

The panel grilled me about my design. I answered their questions, speaking slowly and deliberately. But soon my words started to flow with the inspiration and reasoning behind my senior design project. I knew that although my words to the panel weren't perfect, they were beautiful. I felt it. Everyone in the room felt it.

Then came the announcement that I'll never forget: "Congratulations, Mary, you are this year's winner of the Institute of Electrical and Electronics Engineering Design and Implementation Award!" In that instant, I felt the unique reverence that only a game-changing moment can create. The African had spoken, and people were proud of her. More importantly, I was proud of myself. My confidence soared, knowing that I had something of value to contribute. Later that week, I learned I would graduate number one in my electrical engineering class. Finally, I thought, "You know what? Maybe I can actually become something!" And I did.

My old high school teacher was right. The Easter Bunny and a rocket scientist do have something in common: the unbelievable! Today, I walk through life proud of the African heritage of which I was once ashamed. Who knows what would have become of me had I allowed that class back in South Carolina to crush my dreams forever.

Game Changers have a love affair with their true selves. When you make friends with who you are and do that which is uniquely you, the world will open its doors to you. As you fall in love with who you are supposed to be and what you are supposed to do in this life, you will start to feel a sense of belonging to the bigger mission of our world. You will emanate pure joy and feel inspired, powerful and valuable. There is no competition when it comes to your "you-ness." When you embrace your uniqueness, the only competition becomes how quickly you will triumph.

————

Be ambitious but be realistic. You're not going to achieve every goal the way that you set out to achieve them. Don't be angry or upset at every misstep. Give yourself a lot of room to reflect and find another path. Finding success is about seeing and carving out the path that you really want for yourself and then chasing it down vigorously.

You've also got to have a great sense of humor. I have learned to laugh at myself. A sense of levity has saved me on many occasions. I think positivity and optimism, as warm and fuzzy as they sound, are really important.

—ALEXANDRA CAMERON, CEO OF KEEK INC. AND
FORMER GENERAL MANAGER OF HOT 97

Live Your Life by Design

Do or do not; there is no try.

- YODA, *THE EMPIRE STRIKES BACK* -

I believe that destiny is not something that happens to you, but rather something you create. If you are not living by design, then life is happening to you by default. I came to this realization several years ago as I sat in the back of a limo sent by a major movie studio to pick me up. I was on my way to speak to the head of the studio about how I could help them leverage online technology to distribute their existing content. As we entered the studio lot, I thought of a bus full of employees with pink slips in hand on their way to a job fair that I had run across earlier. I realized then and there that I had designed a career for myself. I was talking with big-time players, from NBC Universal to Amazon.com, as well as companies that were responsible for 70 percent of the music sales globally. Here I was flush with opportunities, while those on the bus—many of whom I'm sure were more talented or intelligent than me—were out of jobs.

Life happens by default or by design. It's completely up to you. Either you allow life to happen to you, or you shape it and mold it in your favor. If you choose to create the life you desire and take action to make it happen, then that's the path that you will be on.

Otherwise, you will live life according to someone else's wishes and desires. When you live without intention, you're like a leaf floating in a stream. You go where the current takes you, whether that's where you want to go or not.

Life happens by default or by design. It's completely up to you.

If you're not living your dreams, chances are you're living your fears, because fear is the only thing that stops one from pursuing their dream. If you're not living the life you've imagined for yourself, then you're settling for a life that is less than what you are capable of. Being a Game Changer starts with a decision to live your life by design rather than by default. There are no accidental Game Changers. Your decisions in life guide you to your choices. If you want to live the life you dream of, you must decide:

1. Who do you want to be?
2. How do you want to pursue your greatness?
3. What will you do to leave your mark on the world?

WHAT IS YOUR "SET POINT"?

Living life with intention starts with the right mind-set, beliefs and attitudes. The life you are living today is the result of your past thoughts and beliefs. So it is extremely important that you become aware of the information you are feeding your mind. The battle of life is truly the battle for the mind. Feed your mind more of what you want to see in your life, and your outcomes will change accordingly. This is especially true when it comes to your thoughts and beliefs about yourself.

Much of our belief system, and subsequently our actions, is based on our self-image. But how does our self-portrait determine our behaviors and ultimately our outcomes in life? In science there is a concept known as a homeostatic system. Homeostatic systems are self-regulating and depend on a pattern of activities to return to a specified condition known as the "set point." A great example of a homeostatic system is the air-conditioning or heating system you have in your home. If the temperature in the room goes above or below the set point of the thermostat, the system automatically turns on or off to return the room temperature to the set point.

Humans are a lot like homeostatic systems. We are *natural regulators* who tend to move in the direction of our set point, and our set point is our self-portrait. Whatever beliefs you have about yourself, your brain will automatically work vigorously to maintain that set point. If you think you are a failure, you will take actions based on failure in order to maintain that set point. For example, if you earn a promotion you don't believe you are worthy of or develop a relationship you don't believe you deserve, you will likely subconsciously do something to sabotage the situation. On the other hand, if you believe you are a winner, you will take actions to maintain that set point. If you see yourself as a highly capable Game Changer, you will act in accordance with success principles until you reach that condition.

How you see yourself drives how you behave. Yet many of us never stop to think about the view we hold of ourselves or how it came to be. In essence, our self-image is imprinted by our past experiences—the good, the bad and the ugly words, actions and people we have encountered throughout our lives. Often our view of ourselves is not based in reality, but we may not even be aware that we're operating based on a faulty self-portrait. This is why it's critical to stop and evaluate how you view yourself. Otherwise, you will always see yourself as others have defined or labeled you and adapt to that definition.

Just as a thermostat must have a set point in order to work properly, your mind also must have a set point. And whether you realize it or not, your mind already has a set point. The question is, what is it? You cannot change until you first know what you believe about yourself. What do you tell yourself about *you*? Is your mantra "I can't . . ."? Or is it "I am capable of doing great things"? If your set point is low (that is, low self-image), and you don't take steps to move it higher, you will likely always struggle to succeed. Game Changers who achieve uncommon success have a high set point, a positive self-image and the firm belief that they can achieve anything they set their mind to.

Creating a more positive self-image is the first step in the journey to becoming a Game Changer. Our environment is constantly bombarding us with negativity. Even the most confident and optimistic among us needs an occasional image boost. A higher self-image feeds the brain a new, positive set of instructions to follow and act on. Here are a few tips for raising your set point:

- Absolutely and positively accept and believe that you have the power to create anything that you can imagine.

- Create and hold in your mind a vivid self-portrait of the person you would like to be. In a perfect world without limitations or restrictions, who would you like to be? What would you feel like, look like, act like? That is your true essence.

- Focus intently on your new set point. Practice thinking about your new self-portrait. You can become a master at the art of belief in self simply by practicing, just as you would do with anything else you want to be good at. Organize your thoughts about yourself so that the positive ones are your dominant focus. Your actions follow the strongest thoughts, so by forcing positive images to the front, you can positively influence your actions.

- Feed your mind with inspirational stories of others who have gone before you and achieved similar dreams.

The way you respond to the world is based on what you've decided to believe about yourself. What you believe you are, you will manifest. It is far better to establish your set point high and continually be striving for greatness rather than have it set too low and dwell in mediocrity. I believe at my core that you are a unique and amazing individual with something incredible to offer this world. Now it's time for you to unleash your potential.

A SURE PATH TO MEANINGFUL SUCCESS

We spend most of our waking hours as adults working. Sadly, far too many people find themselves in jobs or careers that they dislike or that leave them unfulfilled and wonder, "How the heck did I get here?" If you find yourself at work watching the clock, counting the days until Friday and daydreaming of doing something else, you are not living your greatness. To find lasting and meaningful success, you must consciously design and create the career that you want.

A job, career or business is the primary way for you to express your greatness. Your professional endeavors should align with your passion, your potential and your purpose. When you are living your greatness, your work becomes your life's reward—that thing that gives you infinite gratification, joy and fulfillment. If you fail to incorporate your greatness into your everyday life, then you will miss life's greatest reward.

Too often people let life pass them by because they think that they could never make enough money living their greatness or that it would be frivolous to pursue it. While that may be what we have been conditioned to believe, it simply isn't true. Just ask Pinterest founder Ben Silbermann. He was living his life by default. "My parents are doctors, both my sisters are doctors, so I figured I'd just be a doctor too," he told *Inc.* magazine. "Sometime in my junior year [of college], I had this sudden realization that maybe that wasn't for me. I was sort of lost at sea."

After changing majors and graduating from Yale with a degree in political science, Silbermann was working as a consultant when he became intrigued by the technology boom. It was his destiny calling. "I remember I had this feeling that this was the story of my time and I was in the wrong place." Making a major course correction, Silbermann quit his job, moved to Silicon Valley (the tech industry's Mecca) and fought for a job with Google so he could gain a native understanding of the tech industry. I think it's safe to say that, like Silbermann, many people had dreams of making it big in the tech industry, but precious few acted with intention like he did.

The social media phenomenon we know today as Pinterest began in 2009 as an after-hours project between Silbermann, Paul

Sciarra and Evan Sharp. As a child, Silbermann spent many enjoyable hours collecting stamps and insects. Ben came to believe that the things people collect say a lot about who they are and what they value. When he became frustrated at Google because as a nonengineer he wasn't allowed to develop products, his girlfriend told him to stop complaining and go build what he wanted. And what he wanted to create was an interactive website where people could show collections of things they were interested in. "I can't say [Pinterest] came from really hard-nosed business analysis," he told *Inc.* "It was just something I really wanted to see built. I just thought it could be so good for the world if people could share these things about themselves."

Four months after its launch, Pinterest had a scant few hundred users. Nine months after launch, it still had only ten thousand users—a complete failure by most tech start-up standards. True Game Changers that they are, Silbermann and his cofounders understood the value of faith, patience and hustle. "We just felt like if every day we were getting a little bit closer to something that we would be really proud of, we would never regret the time we'd invested." Their efforts were rewarded when Pinterest finally took off . . . exponentially! Three years after its founding, Pinterest was valued at $7.7 billion, and as of this writing, it is one of the fastest-growing social networks. Pinterest beautifully represents the intersection of Ben Silbermann's passions, potential and purpose, and it is proof positive that you can live your greatness *and* make a living doing it.

Pursuing your greatness is a guaranteed path to meaningful success—to a career that will not only pay the bills, but pay the heart as well. Consider the difference between the person who works a job because they have to versus the person who does a job because they are passionate about the work. Which one is going to get ahead? Which one is going to be more creative? Which one is going to work harder, longer, smarter? The one who dreads the work and watches the clock, or the one who loves the work and is passionate about it? Those who work in the center of their greatness achieve uncommon success. When your work aligns with your highest point of contribution, you will naturally climb to new heights and joyfully look for opportunities to do more of what you love to do. The biggest challenge then becomes balancing your life, because you will go to bed reluctantly at night and jump out of bed in the morning with excitement to do that which you enjoy.

If what you're doing doesn't energize you and fulfill you, then you are in the wrong place doing the wrong work. It is possible to create the life you desire, but it doesn't happen by accident. Living your greatness must be your daily focus. Everything you do should move you toward giving your best and highest contribution. Consider the following:

- When you dream of the future, what do you see yourself doing? We are drawn to people, places and situations with high concentrations of opportunities to experience our greatness.

- What would fill you with pride and joy to say? *I am an artist. I am an engineer. I am a singer. I am a teacher. I am a writer. I am a* _____ *(fill in the blank with your greatness).*

- What is your dream job? What would significant, meaningful success look like to you? Envision yourself following your passion and using your gifts and talents.

- Look for organizations that are already addressing a problem related to your purpose and consider going to work for them. Living your greatness doesn't necessarily translate to starting your own business. Early in my career, I was very fulfilled working for Boeing, the Aerospace Corp., Harris Corp. and PanAmSat (a *Newsweek* company).

- Use freelance websites to practice using your passion and potential to serve others or to solve a particular problem. If this kind of work proves to be your best and highest point of contribution, then you can start to build a business around it.

Creating the life and career you desire can be a struggle in the beginning. You may have to endure potential hardships, whether it's rubbing pennies together while launching a business, working three jobs to put yourself through school or giving up the creature comforts of a well-paying job to follow your passion. But it is so worth it. My sister is an attorney who started her career as a prosecutor. She had a phenomenal record and made a good living, but something was missing—a sense of purpose and fulfillment. Through her work as a prosecutor, she often encountered detainees with immigration problems, and she always found herself wanting to help them. After much contemplation, she decided to go into immigration and family law. Despite being a single mother of three, she took the leap to design her life, often studying and working around the clock. Today, she owns a thriving immigration law firm in London and has truly found her highest point of contribution.

Your true passion should drive your work, your career and ultimately your life. Choose to live your life by design by doing what you love rather than doing what is safe. Do not compromise. Let your heart leap and your feet will follow.

RIDE THE WAVE OR GET SWEPT AWAY

I'm going to guess that right now you're probably thinking, "Mary, I would love to follow my passion and do something purposeful in my work, but that's so much easier said than done!" A decade ago, I would have agreed with you, but the world has changed. We are at a time in our history like no other—a time when we are truly limited only by our imagination. Today, technology allows anyone, anywhere—including you—to position themselves in the center of their greatness and take advantage of the right opportunities.

Technology has changed everything about our lives—the way we work, play, communicate and learn. People are tweeting before they can talk and Skyping before they can speak. At just two years old, my son knew how to create art on a tablet.

We have access to massive amounts of computing power, information and data at our fingertips. The average smartphone has more power than all of NASA did in 1969. As of this writing, 91 percent of all people on earth have a mobile phone, and 56 percent of people own a smartphone. There are now more mobile *devices* on earth than there are people. If NASA was able to put a man on the moon with the limited technology they had in 1969, imagine what we can do with that technology today!

Although the first commercial use of the Internet was in 1991, in terms of its ultimate capabilities, it's still a toddler. It is just learning to run, and in the future it will give us capabilities beyond our wildest imaginings. It's difficult enough to fathom what it's already given us up to this point. Just a few decades ago, we had only three major television networks providing news and entertainment for everyone. There are currently some 265 million domains registered, 1 billion websites and 2.58 billion webpages, and the web continues to grow literally by the second. Every URL is in effect a broadcast channel, meaning anyone, anywhere can cultivate an audience. Home videos made for nothing can get more views on the web than TV shows and commercials. Gone are the days of being forced into cookie-cutter tastes determined by a few television executives. The web offers virtually everything and anything that anyone could want, from breaking news to how to safely floss your dog's teeth.

Technology is also driving major changes in the workforce. Today's job seekers are competing with people from around the world, not just in their own country. More and more jobs—from customer service call centers to software development departments—are being outsourced to other countries. In the future, many jobs we know today will be minimized or become obsolete in the same way that ATMs, online banking, self-checkout and online shopping have impacted jobs in banking and retail. As smart machines take over more manufacturing and services jobs, there will be an increasing demand for the kinds of skills machines are not good at. These are higher-level thinking skills that cannot be codified—game-changing skills such as emotional intelligence, imagination, curiosity, creativity and connecting the dots. *People* will have to develop practical solutions to the overabundance of technology and find ways to humanize things again.

You don't have to be a rocket scientist to realize that we are in the midst of a seismic shift. These changes have vast implications for all of us—whether one is an entrepreneur, a manager, a line worker, a student, a teacher, a business, a government or a school. If you think these changes don't affect you, you are flat-out wrong. Everyone will be affected in some way. Once again the question becomes, will you let technology dictate to you, or will you use it to design the career, business and life of your dreams? You can either ride the wave or get swept away. Technology is a huge tidal wave that can take you further than you ever imagined. I say grab your surfboard and let's "hang ten"!

TECHNOLOGY MAKES THE DREAM POSSIBLE

Technology has spawned a whole new world in which you can align your passion, potential and purpose with what you do for a living—and possibly impact our world in a significant way. Opportunities are everywhere, and thanks to technology you have the tools to design the life that you have only dreamed of until now. Essentially, all you need is access to the Internet.

"It's a trite thing to say that the Internet really is changing the world, but there has never been a time in human history when individuals are more empowered than today," Harvard professor Dr. Harry Lewis told me. "A single person sitting alone in their room can write and publish a book. With only the power of an idea, you can start a blog and attract people to it. You can write poetry and share it with other people and get their reactions to it. It's now possible for people to avoid the various kinds of gatekeeping that the corporate world, publishers and other established institutions have perpetuated in the past. So there is an enormous amount of human potential—human creativity empowered—that exists in the world today."

The resources and manpower that used to be available only to the largest enterprises are now available to anyone through collaborative and social technologies. I have a team of designers, programmers and marketers who work together yet are scattered across the globe, with a core team in Florida, and other team members located in Pakistan, Beijing and even in the Himalayas. I have writers and other staff members with whom I've worked for more than a decade but have never met in person, only via Skype. I know colleagues who use virtual administrative assistants to set meetings and take calls from offices on the other side of the world.

Today, you as an individual can access markets that individuals could never have tapped into just ten years ago. Opportunities are overflowing in developing areas without legacy infrastructure such as in South America and Africa. Technology allows us to instantly connect 24/7 with the far reaches of our planet. You can now be a citizen of the world without ever leaving home. The entire world is your backyard, and your work has the potential to reach a massive global audience. Websites like oDesk and Elance offer freelance opportunities for you to test markets and organically grow your business. A company called Envato empowers graphic artists and other techies to sell their work and services globally, and several have reached $1 million in sales. The days of the starving artist are over.

Innovation has provided tools for anyone at any age and with just about any skill level to make a living. Retirees with vast experience and expertise can offer advice and services through the web to people all over the globe. And you don't have to have a technical background to take advantage of technology. HopStop and its founder, Chinedu Echeruo, are prime examples. Chinedu had the vision for the app and found the programmers to make it happen. Technology has even allowed us to globalize compassion.

Antoinette Tuff became an accidental hero when she miraculously persuaded a gunman at a Georgia elementary school to surrender. Shortly after the incident, she created a fund to help inner-city children. Hoping she might get $1,500, she then set up a page on a fund-raising website to collect donations. Within a matter of days, she had received more than $100,000 in contributions.

If you doubt that you can design the life you dream of, meet Micha Kaufman. Micha was an Israeli lawyer with a boring job. He wanted out of his situation and believed he was an entrepreneur at heart. While brainstorming various problems that he wanted to solve with a business, he landed on the idea of creating a website where people could do various tasks for just five dollars. He figured in a recession everyone could use a break. Searching the web, he found a similar site run by Shai Wininger, a Russian living in Siberia who worked in information technology at a bank. Kaufman contacted Wininger, the two teamed up and Fiverr was born.

The premise of Fiverr is global freelancing—the idea that everyone has a talent that someone else needs—and the notion that people can freelance their way to fiscal freedom. Kaufman and Wininger launched Fiverr with the intention to change the freelancing game. They felt that traditional freelancing models were broken and outdated, focusing on the cheapest price rather than the creativity and talent. Fiverr aimed to fix what was broken by building a simple, intuitive and fun marketplace for those who are creative, talented and more efficient, not necessarily for those who compete for the lowest price. Founded in 2010, Fiverr has seen phenomenal growth. More than 1.5 million people use the site to buy and sell services. (Fiverr says a service, called a "gig," is purchased every six seconds.) Members are located in more than two hundred countries, and sellers offer more than 1.8 million gigs in 120 different categories. Kaufman and Wininger are millionaires.

As if this story isn't amazing enough, consider that three years after starting the company, Kaufman and Wininger still had never met in person, only virtually. They built a multibillion-dollar global business together via technology despite living thousands of miles away from each other. Equally interesting is that Kaufman is an entrepreneur with neither technical nor creative skills. And Fiverr wasn't Kaufman's first experience with technology entrepreneurship. While still a lawyer, he developed the idea for a computer securities product that would encrypt data. Lacking coding skills, he searched the web until he found someone with the skills to create it. You don't have to be a technology guru to be a game-changing entrepreneur. All you need is a vision and the willingness to vigorously stalk your dream.

LEAVE YOUR MARK

With six children and my dad's entire extended family dependent on my parents, money was always scarce when I was growing up. As a teenager I went to boarding school, which is common in Ghana. One day while I was preparing to return to school for the next session, I realized that my packed trunk was only half full. I became furious with my father, embarrassed that there wasn't enough food or money to fill my trunk for the entire term. I asked him why he hadn't just stayed in America instead of returning to Ghana and why he wasted so much time working on projects that didn't pay him.

He took me for a walk and explained to me that he lived a very fulfilling and meaningful life. He had afforded us a loving home, food, more than enough clothes and a great education. He spent loads of time with us, playing, telling jokes, dancing, reciting poetry and cheering us on. He acknowledged that he could have stayed in America and worked, but he had returned to Ghana to make a difference, to help restore the country to a democracy. He had worked tirelessly (and for no pay) for the cause, becoming one of the founding members of the New Patriotic Party and later serving as its president.

My father went on to explain that he lived his life the way he did because he wanted to create a legacy. And then he said, "My child . . . in the end, you will be remembered for one of two things: the problems that you create or the problems that you solve. What will you do that will live on long after you are gone?"

Fortunately, he lived to see the first democratic government in Ghana since the coup d'état. He passed away a week after his eightieth birthday from malaria. As thousands of people poured into his funeral to say their farewell, it was the problems he had solved for them that they were most grateful for. My father's legacy was democracy in Ghana, the library he created at the University of Cape Coast, the work he did on behalf of the Catholic Archdiocese, the children he raised to be good citizens and the people whose lives he touched. As I sat there at the funeral, his words about leaving a legacy resonated within the walls of my soul.

Leaving a legacy is about leaving your mark on the world—something that will endure long after the memory of you has faded from people's minds. Without a legacy, you will have squandered the precious gift of life, for you will not have fulfilled your purpose. Without a legacy, what is a person after he or she leaves this world? Nothing, really. Your mission in this life is to do something great with your passion, potential and purpose, and that doesn't always translate into money. Leaving a legacy is not about accumulating wealth. A legacy must be rooted in something purposeful for it to be meaningful.

In many African cultures, the greatness of a man is determined by the number of lives he impacts during his time on earth. Funerals are major events, planned out months in advance like weddings. When the time comes, people share stories of the departed, bring gifts of thanks and put on elaborate plays, for he has touched those people somehow. What will people say at your funeral?

Choose to spend your days doing something meaningful. Don't let them be filled with noise by default. Use your greatness to leave an indelible mark, to leave your corner of the world better than you found it. When you are gone, you will be remembered by the problems that you created or the problems that you solved. Endeavor to find and solve some really good problems with your life, your skills and your passion. Leave your mark on the world.

Find Your Tribe

—————

People who need people are the luckiest people in the world.

- BARBRA STREISAND -

When Barbra Streisand sang that people who need people are the luckiest people, she must have been talking about the formula for game-changing success. Trying to live your passion, potential and purpose without opportunity is a fruitless endeavor, and opportunities come from people. Game Changers are bold enough to stand alone, but also recognize that as humans they have limits. In order to truly effect change and achieve uncommon success, they cannot do it alone. They understand that "1" is not a multiplier. I call the number 1 a mathematical perversity, because no matter what you multiply it by, you end up with the *same* result (10 × 1 = 10). But multiply any number by a number larger than 1, and you get *more* (10 × 2 = 20). The larger the multiplier, the greater the result.

The same concept holds true with people. By yourself, you can only do so much, effect so much change. Add a partner, though, and together you can accomplish more. Form a team, and you can do far more and impact even more people than just the two of you could. And when you enlist the help of a tribe, you can literally change the world, because your efforts—and the efforts of everyone else in the tribe—are multiplied exponentially. Build a tribe and they will help you spread your vision to the farthest-flung places on the globe.

Your tribe represents the people who recognize and speak your language—the language of your vision. They believe in your mission, even if they don't understand it, and will stand with you for the cause. Irrespective of race, ethnicity, religion, age or gender, those who see your brilliance are your tribesmen. It's not about national or geographic borders; it's about purpose. Your tribesmen are not necessarily people who look like you, act like you or even think like you, but rather those who will help you champion and fulfill your promise. Your tribe is your support system—the people who will help you up and dust you off when you fall, the people who can't wait to see you shine brighter than Andromeda.

You will know when you find "your people." It will be a joy to be there. I felt like I had run away and joined the circus when I worked with directors and engineers in digital cinema. Finding your tribe is so important, because that is where "home" is. It's where your greatness lives—among them.

DON'T BE AFRAID TO ASK FOR HELP

While one might think that Game Changers would be fiercely independent, the truth is they are keenly aware of the importance of asking for help. If you're going to dream big, think big and set big goals, you're going to need some help. No one changes the game by themselves. Yet I find that people are often hesitant to ask for and accept help because they are either embarrassed about needing to ask for it in the first place or afraid they will be seen as incompetent or lacking somehow.

To be sure, asking for help is not an easy thing to do. For example, when I had to raise capital for a business venture, there were people who responded as though I were on the streets begging. I stayed positive and pushed through the negativity by thinking of all the other people who had endured similar hardships in making their dreams a reality. When you focus on the big picture ("I need help because I have an outrageously audacious vision and I want to change the world") rather than personalizing the situation ("I need help because I can't handle it on my own"), it's much easier to ask for and receive help.

Alex Cameron advises not to let pride or ego get in the way of success. "I spent a lot of my life trying to do things on my own. I took on a lot of battles and struggles, trying to conquer the world by myself. I probably would have succeeded much faster and much earlier had I been willing—and not been too proud—to ask for help."

Former Staples executive Laurie Clark is also a big believer in seeking support. "Don't be a silo. Don't be the person who thinks, 'I know it all, I can do it all, and I don't want help.' If someone wants to help you, why would you turn that down? I had a CEO at a former company who would give me advice. I would sit there and listen intently because the CEO of the company thought I was important enough to take time to tell me how I can do something better. If someone is trying to help you, take some help and listen! Likewise, don't be afraid to ask for help. If you don't ask, you won't get."

Here are some places you can go to find help and possibly grow your tribe at the same time:

- **Accelerators.** An accelerator is a program or company that helps businesses—mainly start-ups—connect to success. Many accelerators make financial investments, while others provide valuable resources and connections. It's like instant access to a rich and powerful "uncle." Accelerators like Y Combinator have helped start-ups such as Dropbox, Airbnb, Heroku, Reddit and Scribd get off the ground. After hearing a lot about accelerators, I applied for and was accepted into Google's NewME Accelerator. It renewed my interest in asking for help and seeing other perspectives. I recommend that whether you're starting a business or looking for contacts in your area, consider participating in an accelerator in your field. Through these types of programs you will meet actively compassionate mentors, gain insights and develop direct contacts with the right people.

- **Incubators.** Incubators are also great places to find like-minded people who can offer guidance and direction. Incubators usually work with companies, but can also help individuals get into the right career. The main difference between accelerators and incubators is that accelerators are short-term programs to help you launch a business, whereas incubators tend to be long-term programs that provide resources such as shared office space at low or below-market rates.

- **Network.** I have many tribespeople today, but there are some amazingly awesome ones who joined the tribe even before I had the language to articulate my vision. It is fair to say that my life would have been dramatically different if not for these people. They became my advisors and champions of my cause. They guided me, opened countless doors for me, went out of their way to help me, inspired me and connected me to massive opportunities and critical stakeholders. Most of the people who ultimately became my mentors were people I met at industry events, through work and through other tribespeople. These are the people who will help you win the war. But generals are not born on the battlefield; you bring them with you into battle. That is why I can't stress enough the importance of relationships in creating game-changing success.

- **SCORE.** When I first started my company, I went to SCORE (Service Core of Retired Executives), where I met a retired industry executive named Cecil. He helped me create my first business plan and also introduced me to many people. SCORE offers free or very low-cost expert, unbiased business advice to small businesses and start-ups. I found it truly fascinating that this was a completely free service. SCORE offers help online and through 320 local chapters across the United States. There's an African proverb that says when an elder dies, his village loses its library. SCORE is truly a vast library of business wisdom to take advantage of.

The key that unlocks uncommon success is always tied to another hand, and sometimes that help comes from the most unlikely sources. Sam Tarantino is a musician and the cofounder of Grooveshark, a company that combated piracy and changed the music industry paradigm by offering free streaming music. In a video interview with *Inc.* magazine, Sam recalls the most difficult time in his company's history—a time of financial crisis when they couldn't make payroll and were four months behind on the rent. After months of "absolute misery, breaking out in hives and not being able to sleep much," Sam was desperate. In a last-ditch effort to save the company, he went to the landlord for help.

"That is desperation—going to your landlord whom you owe four months of rent to," Sam told *Inc.* "I told him, 'I know we owe you $40,000, *but* . . . if you invest $150,000 [to help us secure this next round of financing], I'll pay the back rent as soon as the financing closes plus three months' rent going forward.' He thought we were crazy."

After giving it some thought, however, the landlord invested the funds needed to take the company off life support and launch it into music history. It turns out it was a good investment. Grooveshark's revenue grew from $3,000 that first year to $5 million just three years later. They have now streamed more than twenty-five billion songs.

You never know where help is going to come from. If you keep working, keep knocking on doors and keep asking, you will find the people who will make a difference in your fate. "Never, never, never give up," Sam said. "Because as long as you stay with it, you never know when luck breaks and something turns your way." And

> You never know where help is going to come from.

when fortune does turn your way, be sure to pay it forward and lend a helping hand to someone else.

FOUNDERS OF THE TRIBE

Most of us can point to a handful of people who made a difference in the trajectory of our life. These people are often the founding members of our tribe. They are the ones who believed in us, saw our potential and imagined the possibilities for us. They lifted us on their shoulders so we could see farther and lovingly kicked us out of the nest when we were ready to fly but afraid to go out into the world on our own. They helped us achieve what we never could have done on our own. Laurie Clark's grandmother was the founder of her tribe. "My grandmother had nothing," she says. "She worked in a sweatshop and scrubbed boards to make extra money for me to have a skate outfit. She would tell me, 'Laurie Anne, you're not going to live like this. You're going to be more than this. You're going to do wonderful things.' I'd feel like a million bucks."

I clearly remember the founders of my tribe. There were my parents, of course, but also the Cody family, who allowed me to stay with them when I first arrived in America, and the Coopers, who took me in while I was in high school and gave me more love than I felt I deserved. A big Game Changer in my life was the engineer who strongly encouraged me to pursue a career in deep space science. I often wonder where my life would be today if I hadn't met that man and if he hadn't uttered those kind words. I wonder if he ever knew how those few minutes of his time led to a lifetime of opportunities for me.

Another early member of my tribe was Lori Hunter, my dean at Syracuse University. She had so much faith in me. I was an engineering student by day and a matchmaker by night. I was also enrolled in the ROTC program, which often required being up at 6:00 a.m. for drills, so I was always lacking sleep. Dean Hunter campaigned on my behalf to create the Academic Excellence Workshop, where students who excelled could get paid to tutor other undergraduate students. The program paid quite well, allowing me to quit one of my jobs and still make enough money to pay for living expenses. Not only did Dean Hunter give me a break, she was also an example of confidence, style and grace.

I like to think of the founding members of our tribe as "early adopters" of our vision. Such was the case with photo-sharing website Flickr and Esther Dyson, a Wall Street technology analyst and angel investor who nurtures start-up ventures. But for the actions of one individual, Flickr might have gone the way of thousands of other technology start-ups—to the graveyard. But that individual wasn't Esther Dyson—at least not initially.

Recent reports indicate that Flickr has more than ninety-two million registered members, but there was a time when founder Catherine Fake was struggling to get the word out about her fledgling business. Back then, one of the best ways to promote a tech start-up was at the influential and high-profile PC Forum. Fake was determined to attend the $5,000-per-attendee conference, but the company was completely out of money. Not to be deterred, she wrote a letter to the head of the conference, Esther Dyson, about attending for free in exchange for presenting a session. Dyson denied her request, but in a surprising turn of events, one of Dyson's staff members said yes. It was at that conference that Catherine met Jerry Yang, a founder of Yahoo!, the company that later purchased Flickr for millions.

"It was one of those situations in which you try to get through the door, try to get through the door, try to get through the door . . . and then you get through the door!" Fake told *Inc.* magazine. Just one person opening the door for another can make all the difference. After learning that one of her staff had allowed the Flickr folks to attend, Dyson reluctantly agreed to meet with Fake and her team. By the end of the meeting, Dyson was ready to invest. Fake recalled, "That was our first breakthrough." Soon after

Dyson committed, so did a number of other investors. Esther Dyson was an early adopter, one of the founders of the Flickr tribe.

You never know who has the keys to let you into the kingdom. It could be the prince, or it could be the butler. No one is too small or too big to affect your life. If not for Esther Dyson's bold assistant, things would have turned out very differently for Flickr. Everyone matters, and the smallest contribution can sometimes make the biggest difference.

THE PEOPLE MAKE THE CULTURE . . .
SO CHOOSE YOUR TRIBESMEN CAREFULLY

Right before Christmas of 2009, just a few months before Sam Tarantino of Grooveshark asked his landlord for an investment, he had to break the news to his staff that the company had run out of funds and couldn't make payroll. In an interview with *Inc.* magazine, Sam said that he expected a mass exit. What happened next was a validation of his choice for tribesmen—not a single soul walked away.

The composition of your tribe—the quality of the people and your relationships with them—will determine in large part how far you go. The people you surround yourself with create your environment, and your environment ultimately affects who you become. It is not a coincidence that certain schools consistently yield game-changing graduates. The environment dictates the type of people that emerge. Founding member of the globally iconic band the Black Eyed Peas, will.i.am is a modern-day Renaissance man who has changed the definition of what it means to be an artist. He is a Game Changer who created a new genre of music that blends funk, electronic and urban formats. As a child, he was bused from the projects to school in Pacific Palisades, the wealthy part of town, giving him access to a better education and a different lifestyle from the gang-infested area he lived in. "You could be the best artist, the best businessperson, but if you have bad friends, you're not going to do anything," he told E! Television's *Pop Innovators*. "Your friends and your ensemble become your uniform."

Entrepreneur and author Jim Rohn is credited with saying, "You are the average of the five people that you spend the most time with." The focal point of the people around you is what seeps into your destiny. When I was in the military and lived in Germany, there were some social groups on base. Two that I found interesting were what I called the Shoppers and the Investors. The Shoppers had fun together spending their paychecks on clothes, furniture, glassware and the like. The Investors spent their time together talking about investment opportunities and new technologies. They invested a good portion of their paychecks in their futures. Unfortunately, the Shoppers with all their new, shiny objects got to me, and I happily emptied my accounts on items such as exquisite marble tables from Italy (which in the end were too expensive to ship back to America). Years later, many of the Investors left the military with sizable nest eggs that allowed them to start businesses or simply retire in style. Two groups of people— same opportunities, different values, very different outcomes.

It is the people that create the culture of your tribe, so you must carefully and deliberately choose who you include. Build your tribe with the right people, and it becomes a currency you can take to the bank. Consider the following:

- Spend time with people before inviting them into the tribe. Make sure you know what they stand for and are clear about their true character, values and intentions.

- Trust your instincts. Remember that brilliant programmer I hired for my company who turned against me? That little voice was whispering to me, but I ignored it. Trust your gut and choose carefully.

- Find people who will fuel your vision. Think about how their focal point will magnify or diminish your mission and ultimately your path in life.

- Choose tribesmen who push you to be better.

- Surround yourself with a network of encouraging people. Their support will make the journey more bearable, even if it's nothing more than a couch to crash on or a shoulder to lean on.

People matter. The people you trust and surround yourself with make all the difference in your life. There is an urban legend about the president and first lady of a certain country visiting the first lady's hometown. As they sat eating, a beggar approached their table to ask for money, and the first lady began chatting with him. When he left, the president inquired as to how she knew the beggar. She indicated that he was her high school sweetheart—the man she almost married. The president said, "You are a very lucky lady. If you had married him, today you would be a beggar's wife instead of the first lady." She looked at the president, smiled and said, "No, if I had married him, today he would be the president!" The most important person you will choose for your tribe is your significant other—the person you let into your inner sanctum. *Choose wisely.*

ATTENUATORS AND AMPLIFIERS

Your tribe either diminishes or enhances your vision, depending on the people you choose. As an engineer, I tend to think of people as either attenuators or amplifiers. In engineering, an attenuator is a device that reduces the amplitude, or power, of a signal, while an amplifier increases the power of a signal. Human attenuators reduce your power and ability to live your greatness, while amplifiers increase your power and ability. Attenuators are subtractors and dividers; amplifiers are adders and multipliers.

Attenuators are negative people who subtract from who you are, shrink your strengths and often divide your team. Have you ever dealt with someone negative and afterward had an instant headache or bout of depression or felt completely drained? That is because negativity is a strong energy force that affects us physically, mentally and emotionally. Attenuators are human Bermuda Triangles who suck the energy and life force out of us.

Attenuators come in all varieties, from well-meaning doubters to malicious saboteurs. Some negative people are simply nonbelievers who come from a place of genuine love and concern. These people might even tell you that your dream is impossible, not because they have no faith in you, but because they simply can't imagine anyone doing it. Other people's sole aim is to deprive others of joy. There are the naysayers who will tell you you're crazy and the critics who will find fault with everything you do. Gatekeepers will flat out try to get in your way and keep you from people who are awaiting your gifts. People of the crabby variety are those who are insecure about themselves, feel threatened by you and will try to pull you down. Thieves will take, take, take from you without offering anything of value in return. And dream snatchers will belittle your *dream*, while haters will belittle *you* just to make themselves feel better.

Amplifiers are essential in your tribe. Amplifiers add to who you are, multiply your strengths, increase the power of your vision and expand your reach. These are the people who believe in you; their vision for the world aligns with yours. Amplifiers are the base of your support system. They are always there to lend a helping hand and support you no matter what. Champions and cheerleaders, coaches and mentors, even heroes are all amplifiers. I wrote this book to be an amplifier for you, to be your cheerleader and hopefully a coach. My mission has been to share with you my experiences, discoveries and beliefs, and to give you the encouragement to keep moving so that you can reach your dreams and goals faster.

A champion is your personal "flag bearer." This person not only believes in you, but also has the resources to connect you to opportunity. Cheerleaders help you get through the fear, pain and doubt that come hand in hand with challenges and setbacks. Game Changers make it not because they never tire or want to give up, but because they have cheerleaders. In the case of WhatsApp founder Jan Koum, it was his caring friend Brian Acton who reached out to him when his mother died. Acton later became WhatsApp's cofounder. When Koum was ready to give up on the business and go get a job, Acton encouraged him to believe in their dream. "You'd be an idiot to quit now," he said. "Give it a few more months."

A coach is someone with whom you can share ideas and be completely vulnerable and truthful, without fear of judgment. The best coaches are part therapist and part guide. Mentors are a great way to learn directly from those who have gone before you. You can meet mentors through industry networking events. Look for people who are where you want to be in the future and try to establish a mentoring relationship with them. If that's not possible, study their successes and their mistakes through books, speeches, blogs and videos.

Heroes inspire you to be your best possible self; they provide inspiration by example. My mother is one of my heroes. She's one of the smartest people I know, and I loved the freedom she had as an entrepreneur. In spite of only having a high school diploma, she established a successful business in Ghana improving supply chain management for rural farmers. Some of my other heroes include Oprah, Bill Gates, Larry Page, Maya Angelou, Nelson Mandela, Rene Anselmo, Steve Jobs, Simon Cowell and Angelina Jolie. In times of struggle, I often ask myself, "What would my hero do in this situation?"

Your tribe can be very empowering or very limiting, depending on the people you choose. Add amplifiers, and do whatever you can to avoid or eliminate attenuators. (Also, be wary of fair-weather friends who appear to support you but won't show you love when the chips are down. They are attenuators in disguise.) Adding amplifiers to the tribe tends to push the attenuators out. It is the law of displacement—the entry of light forces the exit of darkness. Light and darkness cannot coexist.

Use how you feel as a barometer for the people you let into your tribe. Do you feel uplifted or drained after each encounter? Any time you feel down after an interaction you know something is awry. When you have an interaction with someone, it is rare that you remember verbatim their words, but what you don't forget is how you felt. I recently heard from a man who was a bully in high school and taunted me relentlessly just because I was from

Africa. He sent me an invite on Facebook and congratulated me on my accomplishments. Even after all these years, I was immediately thrown into how I felt each time he taunted me. How people make you feel is cast like dye on clothing; it might fade but is never erased completely.

IT'S A SMALL WORLD AFTER ALL

It's a small world and only getting smaller, thanks to technology. People are more connected than ever before. You've probably heard the theory of six degrees of separation—the idea that you are just six people away from any other person on the planet. The theory has been tested several times, including research by Microsoft and a recent study of Facebook data by the University of Milan, which indicates that the separation has shrunk to just 4.74 degrees thanks to social media. An experiment I conducted with five different LinkedIn projects featuring five hundred or more people also showed an average of three degrees of separation to anyone in the connected world.

Social media has brought us closer than ever. Think of the magnitude of having such an infinite Rolodex. I am currently working with Daryl Jones, a Florida senator. While going through his photos during his campaign for governor, I noticed in one picture a certain young man from Chicago who today is president of the United States. Former president Bill Clinton is also a friend of Daryl's. While Clinton was president, he called Jones to ask if he had any suggestions for attorney general. Daryl was working with Janet Reno at the time and recommended her to Clinton, indicating that she was firm, fair, qualified and, most importantly, loyal.

Reno became the first woman to serve as attorney general and the second-longest-serving attorney general to date.

You never know who you know that might be connected to the person that's going to change the course of your life. My cofounders at Gen2Media, Mark Argenti and Ian McDaniel, are also founders of one of the most successful production companies in the business, Media Evolutions. (Mark and Ian also pioneered the game-changing video playback technology that is now widely viewed as the industry standard for use in live concert and stage production.) In the early days of his career, Mark was a genius digital artist who also loved doing audio and video production. But he didn't have a way to channel his passions at work. So in his off time, he did production and stage work through his own company. It was during this time that he happened to meet Steve Fatone, brother of Joey Fatone of *NSYNC fame, who worked in production at Universal Studios.

Before long, Mark became known throughout production circles as the go-to guy for video, audio and graphics. When Joey Fatone was recruited to join *NSYNC, Steve Fatone, having seen Mark's work, knew exactly who to get to do their video and introduced Mark to the band. At the time, Justin Timberlake was dating Britney Spears, who saw Media Evolutions's work and also decided to engage them. One introduction after another led to work with U2, Ozzy Osbourne, the Black Eyed Peas, Will Smith, John Mayer and many other artists. Mark has told me that just before he met Steve Fatone, he was a stagehand doing the backbreaking work of pulling and carrying "the red carpet" for various productions. Within months, he was walking the red carpet himself and flying to Ireland to work with U2.

What if Mark hadn't said hi to Steve Fatone and started a conversation with him? Steve would never have known what a great producer and director Mark was, and Mark would have missed his fate without even knowing it. Everyone you know or meet is a potential tribesman or a connector to a potential tribesman, so treat everyone with respect and dignity. You never know where your tribesmen will come from or when they will appear.

DRAW A BIGGER CIRCLE

One of my mentors is a woman who broke down the good ol' boys club in the Republican Party and became a speechwriter for President Ronald Reagan. I once asked her how she survived the naysayers and critics who called her crazy. She said, "He who drew a circle to keep me out, I drew a bigger circle that kept him in." What she meant was that there will be people who will try to build walls to keep you out and to prevent you from attaining your dreams. But the same walls that are meant to keep you out also limit those who are on the inside. Their world is finite, whereas yours is full of infinite possibilities. By keeping you on the "outside," they open up the entire world for you to search for other opportunities.

If someone is pushing you out or keeping you out, don't be discouraged. It is simply a "no" letting you "know" that this is not your tribe. Don't take disrespect personally, and don't let it stop you. Instead, let it drive you to find your tribe and force you into creating something new. You can't give up just because someone excludes you from a seat at the table inside the circle. As will.i.am says, "You can't let someone else's closed mind close your doors." Start your own picnic—outside. Rather than conform to the rules of their table, you get to write your own rules. You can run free and have cupcakes and champagne for breakfast, lunch and dinner if you want.

That's what Game Changers do—if someone writes the rules to keep them out, they simply create something new or change the game altogether. Oprah chose not to live by the rules of news broadcasting. She was meant for something much bigger where she could be free to be herself. Other newscasters couldn't escape the club they kept her out of. WhatsApp's Jan Koum was turned down for a job at Facebook. If they had hired him, he would have been on the inside, probably coding and getting all sorts of pushback for his ideas. Instead, being excluded put him on the outside to draw a bigger circle—a circle that got so big that a threatened Facebook decided to buy WhatsApp for a cool $19 billion. When your light becomes blindingly bright, people can't help but notice. Success often puts the critics and those who missed your vision to shame. Sometimes, family and friends will not share your passion or see your vision. If that is the case, you have to expand your circle to find those who do. Once your vision comes to life, everyone seems to come back around, including those who weren't around when you needed them the most.

If you start to face opposition where you are, it means you have outgrown the situation. It's time to move on and expand your circle. When Tony Fadell came up with the idea for what would later become the iPod—the device that changed the personal electronics industry and the way we consume music, the most successful consumer electronics product in history—the company he was working for turned the project down. This set him free to shop the concept around. He found a believer in Steve Jobs, went to work for Apple and was able to develop a complete iPod/iTunes solution.

Alex Cameron started to get pushback in her native land of radio, but that dynamic opened up a whole new world that's even bigger than where she was before. Now, as the CEO of Keek, she oversees one of the largest video social networks, with sixty-seven million users. When you are cut free, it sets you free to move toward where you're supposed to be.

People often say to me, "You're a woman and you're black—do you face a lot of discrimination?" My answer is simple: "I don't stay where people don't value what I have to offer. I seek out people and places where my skills and talents are needed and valued." If a person, group or company has no use, need or value for what you have to offer, you're in the wrong place. When you are in the wrong tribe, your difference and your greatness will not be appreciated or valued. It's like being a square peg forced into a round hole. Never stay where you are not valued. Your weaknesses will multiply and your strengths will diminish.

> Never stay where you are not valued.

Alex Cameron wisely said, "You've got to find your place in the world. People are going to put you in a place until you decide what place you want to have." You don't belong everywhere, but you belong somewhere. Where you belong is where your gems will be valued, cherished, loved and appreciated. Know who you are and where you belong. Find that place and find your people, and your genius will thrive.

Start Where You Are

You remake yourself as you grow and as the world changes.
Your identity doesn't get found. It emerges.

- REID HOFFMAN -

Hopefully by now you've realized that most Game Changers are everyday people who went on a journey to live their greatness and be of service to others, with fame and fortune as a by-product. No one starts at the top of the mountain. Everyone has to start at the bottom and climb.

In researching and interviewing more than one hundred Game Changers, I noticed many patterns. A couple of key similarities among all of them were that they never made excuses or let their circumstances stop them. If you intend to live your greatness, you can't wait for the perfect time, the perfect situation or the perfect circumstances . . . they will never come. You will leave this earth waiting to live your greatness, squandering the passion, potential and purpose within you. Start *now* from wherever you are—no matter where that might be—to live your life by design and offer your highest and greatest self.

DON'T LET YOUR CIRCUMSTANCES
DEFINE YOUR CAPABILITIES

In 2010, my life was near picture-perfect. I owned a successful multimillion-dollar company serving high-profile clients, I was passionate about my work and I could see the flashing lights of my ship arriving full of treasure. On top of that, I was engaged to be married. But within a matter of months, I found myself in the center of a storm with everything spiraling down into mayhem. I was voted out of my own company in which I had invested my life's savings, lost everything I had worked so hard for (including my home) and broke off my engagement. I went from being on top of the world with a bright future to a single mother with no income by the time my son was born.

Down to nothing, I was hurt, disappointed and angry at myself and at the people and circumstances that had led me to this point. But I was not defeated. I made a conscious decision not to become embittered. I looked at the bright side of my circumstances—I had family that I could live with. So I packed up my bags and headed to my older sister's house in London. For months, my sister and her family graciously and lovingly took care of us. I used the downtime as an opportunity to rest and reenergize—to spend time with my new son and to reflect on what I wanted to do next, how I wanted to do it and what I would do differently. After a few months, however, I realized I was getting too comfortable. I knew I had to get up and soldier on. I had to start over—from scratch.

Was it tough? Absolutely. It was one of the toughest periods in my life. But I have never defined my capabilities or my opportunities by my circumstances. In fact, looking back at my childhood, even during those times when we had no food and had to borrow from neighbors, I never saw myself as poor. I have never allowed anything to stifle my creativity and curiosity to learn. I never let the fact that I was sixteen and had to leave everything I'd ever known keep me from traveling to America to create a better life for myself. I never let the fact that I was a fry cook at McDonald's stop me from working toward something bigger. So really, why should this time be any different? Why should I let the fact that I had lost my life's savings, was without a home and was now a single mother stop me from offering my best and highest self? I was still the same person, with the same skills and the same dreams . . . bruised, but not damaged.

Game Changers do not define themselves, their abilities or their potential by their circumstances or advantages (or lack thereof). They don't allow lack of money, lack of education, race, gender, age or any other excuse to stop them from doing what they know to be right. Marc and Shanon Parker said of their first game-changing vehicle: "In the beginning, we were working with so little. We had like a fifty-dollar budget, some hand tools we had borrowed and scrap materials that we had scrounged up to build that first bike." Game Changers start where they are and make magic with what they have.

> Game Changers start where they are and make magic with what they have.

Fashion pioneer Eileen Fisher never let her circumstances dictate what she could and couldn't do. As she explained to *Inc.*, "When I decided to go to college, my dad said, 'Well, Eileen, since we don't have the money to send all the kids to school, we have to save up for your brother. He'll need an education to support his

family one day.' It didn't upset me—it was the times. I never expected a penny from my parents. I paid my way through the University of Illinois working as a waitress."

In college, Fisher was a math major until she got a D in calculus. She simply changed her major to interior design. After college,
while working for a design firm, she became frustrated by clothes
and shopping. She wanted to wear comfortable clothes that
worked in the real world, quite unlike the clothes that most
fashion designers were creating. She purchased a sewing machine
and tried her hand at creating some pieces, with mixed results.
But she wasn't deterred. "In my mind I kept seeing simple shapes
made with good fabric." When a friend offered her his booth at a
trade show, Fisher seized the opportunity.

Although she didn't know how to sew and had only $350 in
the bank (and three weeks' lead time), she pulled it off. Before
long, she had $40,000 worth of orders. There was just one prob-
lem: She didn't have the money to buy the materials to fulfill the
orders. After the bank turned her away, she borrowed money from
friends and filled the orders in batches.

Today, Fisher employs nine hundred people and sells her line
in sixty Eileen Fisher stores as well as top-tier department stores.
In yet another game-changing move, several years ago Fisher sold
the company to her employees through an ESOP (employee stock
ownership plan). It was a beautiful example of active compassion.
For Fisher there were a lot of things more important than the
money she could have made from taking the company public or
selling to another design house. "[The company] will be owned by
the people who have put their blood, sweat and tears into it, by the
people who love it and care about it and are thinking about it," she
told *Inc.* Eileen Fisher made a decision to live her life by design

and be the change she wanted to see in the world, and she never let her circumstances dictate her future.

So what happened to me? I picked myself up, dusted myself off, got focused and got back on my grind again. I began contacting people in my tribe, and soon I was considering job opportunities from several top media and retail companies. Ultimately, I decided to revitalize my technology solutions company, Next Galaxy Media (which had been lying dormant), raised a million dollars and launched a new project. Today, under Next Galaxy Media, I'm surrounded by a fantastic, loving team, working on augmented and virtual reality content for Google Glass and Oculus Rift.

> Don't let your situation define who you are and what you can accomplish.

Don't let your circumstance determine your worth or your future. I'm not saying ignore the facts of your situation and have blind hope. I'm saying don't let your situation define who you are and what you can accomplish. Don't let what you see with your eyes limit what you see with your mind and your heart.

TURN YOUR "BUTS" INTO "ANDS"

Too often people look at their circumstances and use them as reasons not to succeed. When we make excuses, we are really saying, "I'm willing to settle for less than I can be." We go through life with a big "but" in front of every dream or goal. "I'd like to do X . . ."

- But I don't have the money.
- But I'm too old.

- But I'm too young.

- But I'm a woman.

- But I have no college degree.

- But I don't know anyone.

- But I'm not smart enough.

- But is it even worth it?

- But I can't do it!

- But I don't think it's possible.

The "but" I hear most often has to do with lack of money. Money is just one of many tools and resources for success, and most of the others can't be bought—acquiring knowledge, building your tribe, using your creativity, outlining a business plan, learning from mentors. Especially today with all the ways to finance one's passions (loans, crowd funding, networking, people donating their talents), money shouldn't be an issue.

> You can make excuses or you can make magic. It's your choice.

Game Changers do not walk through life with big "buts" in front of their vision. They find ways to turn those "buts" into "ands." Rather than "I would love to start a business, *but* I can't because I'm a single parent," the mantra becomes "I'm a single parent, *and* I would love to start a business." You can make excuses or you can make magic. It's your choice.

No matter where you are now, no matter where you've been,

you can start where you are and make a change. In my novel *A Song for Carmine*, the main character comes to a point in his life when he declares, "I will look at the past, but I will not stare at it." This is the toughest thing for many people to do—to look at their past and the circumstances that have led to where they are today and still believe that they can create a future that is vastly different. They believe that their past and present dictate their future. It's simply not true. No one knows that better than Sandra Peart, former Canadian trade commissioner.

Sandra's childhood was filled with chaos and marred by alcoholism, repeated domestic violence, absent parents and homelessness. "Significant events happened in my life that were game-changing for me—some positive, some negative," she told me. "My mom came home one day and said she was headed to the airport. She said she was going to America. I was ten years old. I thought she was going on vacation. She left and I didn't see her again until I was fifteen."

After that, Sandra and her two sisters lived with her grandmother, constantly bouncing from one desperate situation to another—at times homeless, at times living in a plywood and zinc tenement and at times living in a one-room house with three adults and eight children. "Through everything, my sisters and I never ever missed a day of school. Not one!" She went on to explain, "As a child growing up in Jamaica, education was very important. Throughout my entire life that was stressed—no matter what your circumstances, no matter what's happening in life, you stay in school and do well."

Sandra's story is similar to mine in that at the age of sixteen, she came to America looking for a better life. She earned a degree in industrial engineering from Rutgers University and was recruited out of college by IBM. Since then, she has had a long and successful career, leading the way for women in traditionally male-dominated industries. I asked Sandra how her circumstances had shaped and impacted her life. "It definitely made me tough. When you've been through all of that, there isn't much that people can throw at you that you can't get through.

"Having gone through all those adversities made me stick to whatever I put my mind to," she continued. It gave me a focus, hunger and drive because I knew that I did not want to ever go back to [those circumstances]. I also knew that when I had children, I didn't want them to grow up in that kind of circumstance, so I had to find a way to make sure they got a good start."

Time after time throughout her life, Sandra refused to allow her circumstances to dictate her future. Instead, she turned her "buts" into "ands" and turned her life's sour, bitter lemons into sweet lemonade.

A WOUNDED DEER LEAPS HIGHEST

Emily Dickinson wrote in one of her poems, "A wounded deer leaps highest." So often in life, pain is a much stronger motivator than the desire for joy. If you are facing difficult or painful life circumstances, don't use them as an excuse to wallow in self-pity and dwell in mediocrity. Use your challenges to fuel your fire and drive your hustle to live your greatness.

When I interviewed artist Alberto Ruiz for *One2One* magazine, he recalled how his painful childhood forged his character. "Running the streets as a kid in a third-world country without parents (my father bailed out when I was two, and my mother left Ecuador to find work in New York City when I turned eight) cannot possibly be good for a shy, sensitive child of the artistic kind. But it was perfect for a hyperactive freak. Fending for yourself in a hostile environment forces you to think outside the box and to wear many hats. It gave me the passion and the work ethic of a turn-of-the-century immigrant. No job is below me, nothing is too difficult and I have zero tolerance for laziness. I seek independence at all costs. I appreciate life and live every day as if it were my last."

Although she later developed groundbreaking innovations in the field of ophthalmology, Game Changer Dr. Patricia Bath was not initially welcomed by her peers. "I simply wanted to be included in the game, but 'they' didn't even want me to play," she told me. "The rules of the game were designed to exclude women, exclude minorities and exclude the poor, and I was all three."

When I asked Dr. Bath how she was able to win at a game where the odds were stacked against her from the outset, she said, "My brain and psyche had not been schooled in the playbook of defeat and mediocrity. I was so stimulated, challenged and irritated by exclusion and disrespect that a powerful fire grew within me to succeed. When you are faced with a hurdle, you don't simply jump over . . . you jump higher. And perhaps on that day, your jump is the highest."

CHOOSE TO SEE OPPORTUNITIES
RATHER THAN LIMITATIONS

There is a story about two shoe salesmen who were sent to a remote part of Africa. Once they got to their destination—a village of thirty thousand inhabitants—they were told that no one wore shoes in that culture. One of the salesmen left on the first plane out of the country, vowing to quit his company for sending him to a place where no one wore shoes. The second salesman called and thanked his boss for the opportunity to sell thirty thousand pairs of shoes.

In life we are limited by what we imagine our boundaries to be. Some people dwell in self-limiting beliefs and accept whatever life throws their way. Others see the world as full of possibilities and believe they can accomplish whatever they wish. Game Changers like Sandra Peart see opportunities where others see limitations. After several years working for various engineering companies, she applied for the position of trade commissioner for the government of Canada at their consulate in Miami, with responsibilities for the IT, aerospace and defense industries.

Many people would have concluded they weren't qualified for the job and never even applied. I asked Sandra what gave her the confidence to go after the position. "I looked at that job description, and it was intriguing to me. I had never been a trade commissioner before, but when I looked at what the position would be doing, I saw something interesting and new for me to learn. I said to myself, 'I am not going to take myself out of the game. Let them turn me down. I can do that job and do it better than anyone else.' I kind of secretly dared and challenged them to tell me otherwise."

She beat out 120 other candidates to get the job. "I had the IT background and the business background, but they also looked at the challenges that I had been through in life. That led them to believe that I could take on whatever challenges came my way on the job, not give up and find a way to get it done."

When you train your mind to look for opportunities, you will start seeing possibilities that you were blind to before. When I became pregnant, all of a sudden the world seemed to be full of pregnant women. It's the same principle. The mind filters information based on what you are focused on. Your mind also acts like a magnet, attracting the opportunities, resources and people that are necessary to take you in the direction you want to go. In life you can choose to see limits or see opportunities . . . to focus on constraints or on possibilities. Why not choose to succeed rather than to fail before you even get started?

TAKE SMALL STEPS

No matter your passion, potential or purpose, there is a means to make living your greatness a reality. No matter your circumstances, you can always take small steps toward your destination. How did Jan Koum go from living on food stamps to selling WhatsApp for $19 billion? Small steps. How did Eileen Fisher go from a math major putting herself through school to becoming an iconic New York fashion designer? Small steps. How did Laurie Clark go from the projects to Harvard Business School to being one of the first female executives at Staples? Small steps. "Every little accomplishment builds more confidence," Laurie told me. "So I focused on every little win. Little milestones like that go a long way."

In my experience, people on the journey to success often get tripped up because they can't see the entire path or route from where they are now to where they want to be, so they just never start. They worry about all the possible different scenarios and how everything will play out and let those uncertainties about the future stop them from moving forward. You don't have to know how the whole journey will roll out; you just have to take the next small step and the next one and the next one. It's like the navigation system on your car or smartphone that gives you step-by-step directions to your destination. Typically, you don't see the entire route, only the next step. It's okay to not know all the turns ahead. Just trust that it is leading you on the right path to reach your destination. In his book *The Zahir*, Paulo Coelho says, "All you have to do is to pay attention; lessons always arrive when you are ready, and if you can read the signs, you will learn everything you need to know in order to take the next step." Trust that when the pupil (you) is ready, the teacher will arrive.

Today, begin the process of deciding what dream, hope or desire you are going to make a reality, and let everything you do every day from now on move you closer to it. Step by step, start walking toward that person you want to be and that life you want to have. Here are a few small steps you can take to get started:

- **Leverage your day job.** Proactively ask to get involved in projects and assignments that revolve around your passion, potential or purpose. One of my strengths is helping people find and leverage their best assets. The most meaningful compliments I get are from people who have worked for me telling me how much they have grown or honed in on their greatness. One particular former employee comes to mind. When he came to work for me he was a great motion graphics artist. He told me he was very interested in coding and had tinkered with it from time to time, but hadn't had the opportunity to use it in a meaningful way. Knowing that, I assigned him to projects that would allow him to grow his coding skills exponentially, and today he is a phenomenal programmer. He is so incredibly good at what he does, people are amazed to discover he didn't start out as a coder.

- **Start something on the side that revolves around your passion, potential or purpose.** You may not be ready or able to give up your day job and start a new venture. You can dip your toes into the water of your greatness by doing contract work, doing projects through freelance websites, a part-time job or even a weekend internship. Pierre Omidyar famously started eBay as a side experiment while he worked his day job. "For me it was an experiment," he told the Academy of Achievement. "I wanted to create an efficient market where individuals could benefit from participating in that efficient market, kind of level the playing field. And I thought, 'Gee, the Internet, the web, it's perfect for this.' . . . It was just an idea that I had, and I started it as an experiment, as a side hobby basically, while I had my day job. And it just kind of grew. Within six months it was earning revenue that was paying my costs. Within nine months the revenue was more than I was making on my day job, and that's kind of when the lightbulb went off. 'Knock, knock, knock. You've got a business here, do something about it.' So that's when it really started."

- **Look for and apply to jobs in the area or field you're interested in.** You might have to start with an entry-level position or take a pay cut, but you will gain invaluable experience, learn about the industry and find out where the opportunities are.

- **Become a student of your area of interest.** Read books in this area, take classes and start building your skills. I started my first novel, *A Song for Carmine*, a few years ago, writing one chapter at a time. It was trial by fire. But as time passed, I learned more about writing and developed my style. I found editors and people in the industry who guided me through the process. With *A Song for Carmine* completed and published, I'm already thinking about my next project—a sci-fi trilogy that I hope to eventually develop into a game.

Small steps taken consistently will take you farther down the road than you can even imagine right now. You will pick up speed with time; you just have to trust the process. Look for opportunities to apply your greatness in your current situation, then start something on the side, and when that business is big enough to support you, take the plunge. I went back to work several times before finally making the leap to start my own company. It's all about consistent progress. Every step leads to the next, and truly no one has any idea where they will end up.

In the television show *Oprah & Eckhart Tolle: A New Earth*, Eckhart Tolle talks about how the pursuit of greatness is a paradox. "So many people have this idea, 'I want to achieve something great, or be somebody great,'" he tells Oprah. "And they neglect the step that leads to greatness. They don't honor *this step at this moment* because they have this idea of some future moment where they are going to be great."

The foundation for greatness, Tolle says, is "honoring the small things of the present moment." For example, he didn't set out to write a book that would change world consciousness. He simply started by putting pen to paper and then taking the next step. "It's all a sequence of very small moments, and by being true to the small moment, something great arises."

SUCCESS IS A PROCESS OF GROWTH

Most people mistakenly believe they can't make a significant difference with their lives because they think only geniuses, supertalented people or those born with privilege do amazing things. They look at their dreams and think, "How could I possibly do this? It's a fantasy." They don't realize that success is a process of growth.

Every monumental achievement in existence today started as an idea that someone had the courage to pursue. Every high achiever started somewhere and grew their way to the top. The Game Changers discussed in this book didn't start out thinking they were going to change the world; they just went on a journey to fulfill their dreams. We never know where the journey will take us. The only guarantee is that what happens is likely to surprise you. I set out to come to America—a very simple dream, to get from Ghana to America. I ended up as a deep space engineer, rocket scientist, matchmaker, magazine publisher, novelist and so much more.

I believe the reason people make excuses for not pursuing their dreams is they look at the "final product" of what others have created or have become and think they could never attain that level of success. Beneath every excuse is a lack of faith and the fear that they don't have the ability, the skills or the talent to achieve what they truly desire. But that is faulty logic, because they are comparing themselves at the starting point of their journey to someone who has worked years to perfect their skills and hone their craft. It's like comparing a baby to a full-grown man. Give that baby time to grow and develop, and soon enough he will be full-grown too.

We take notice of Game Changers after years of hustle and hard work. If we had seen them when they started, we might never have known they were a Game Changer in the making. If you look at John Mackey today and what he has accomplished, you would never guess where he started. As the co-CEO of Whole Foods Market, he oversees one of the largest and most successful natural and organic food supermarket chains in the country. But in 1978, he was a twenty-five-year-old college dropout, living in his small natural foods store in Austin, Texas.

My personal trainer looks like Ms. Fitness USA. I used to look at her and think I could never be that toned and lean. Then she showed me a picture of herself after she had her third child. I was shocked at the difference. Looking at her now, after years of training, it had never occurred to me that she might have once struggled with her weight.

As you grow along your journey, you're going to be surprised at the things you accomplish. There will be some trial and error in the beginning, but as you go higher, you will gain more perspective. You will find everything you need along the way to be successful and to achieve your dreams—you will meet the people, you will acquire the skills, you will find the tools, you will know when to change course. Ultimately, you will have the ability to create the life you desire.

Much like a newborn baby, you and your dream will grow into something beautiful with nurturing and unrelenting pursuit. If you have the dream, you have within your reach everything you need to make it a reality.

THE NEXT BEST TIME IS NOW

In a *Time* magazine interview, Google founder Larry Page indicated, "It takes ten or twenty years to go from an idea to something being real. We should shoot for the things that are really, really important, so ten or twenty years from now we have those things done." Greatness won't be achieved overnight. It takes time, often years if not decades. The longer you wait to start, the longer it will be until you reach your dreams and goals.

When Kiva.org cofounder Jessica Jackley was asked by the Stanford Graduate School of Business what advice she would give other entrepreneurs, she said, "Start! I meet so many individuals who have great plans, but they take way too long to do anything about them. Just put something out there. It will be imperfect. The real work is in figuring out how to make it better. Wake up each day and say, 'Now what?'"

You have to start from some place at some time, and that place and time is here and now. It's never too late to have the life you were meant to live. For those who think their boat has left, I share the proverb, "The best time to plant a tree was twenty years ago. The next-best time is now."

Always believe. You have to believe that it is possible, even when you don't see it, even when it seems like it's not going to work out. You have to believe that you can do it. You have to believe that it is yours. As you achieve things, you learn more and your horizons expand. You see possibilities that you weren't even aware of before. As you conquer each milestone, you begin to think, "What else can I do?" And you try something else. That added exposure opens up new possibilities, and you start reaching for more things.

"Believe" is the key word. All the other things are important too—you have to work hard, you have to focus, you have to be dedicated. But at the end of the day, if you don't believe that what you want is possible and that you can achieve it, I don't think it will happen. A lot of people work hard and don't achieve what they set out to achieve because they don't believe they can.

—SANDRA PEART, FORMER TRADE COMMISSIONER
FOR THE GOVERNMENT OF CANADA

DARE TO DO SOMETHING GREAT

Do not go where the path may lead, go instead where there is
no path and leave a trail.

- RALPH WALDO EMERSON -

Do you believe that you are worthy of making a significant contribution to the world? So many people settle in life because they
believe that they aren't capable of doing something extraordinary.
I believe you were made for greatness, and when you accept the
challenge to find and live that greatness, you have the potential to
become extraordinary.

Game Changers are simply dreamers who readily answer the
call to explore, to learn, to be more, to do more, to give more. If
you picked up this book and have read to this point, then I know
that you have heard that call. Now I dare you to do something
about it. I dare you to become a Game Changer. I dare you to do
something great with your life—to be more than you ever thought
possible and to participate in the creation of your future and our
future together. I dare you to become a change catalyst . . . to
dream audacious dreams . . . to begin a joy revolution . . . to become a compassionate expression of humanity . . . and to rid the
world of some measure of pain, apathy and isolation.

My favorite part of any sporting event is when the players are just about to enter the arena. The crowd noise is deafening, the anticipation and excitement gripping. The contenders stand on the precipice, the outcome of the game uncertain—the potential for greatness juxtaposed with the possibility of defeat. That is where you are right now. You have stepped into the arena and are now a contender to become the champion of your life. The chants of the critics—as well as the noise of your own doubts, fears and uncertainties—may be deafening. Block it all out and focus on the task ahead of you. Hold your head up high and sashay into the arena as if the outcome is certain.

The game of life is single elimination, "one and done," so you better play to win. It takes heart, audacity and sheer guts and determination to become a champion. You must be willing to take risks and get uncomfortable. As Noah Graj says, "Where your comfort zone ends is where life begins." You need to know that there will come a time when you will have to make tough choices. Keep in mind that every journey of significance requires a measure of sacrifice, which must not be mistaken for loss. Any sacrifice is well worth a lifetime of living with meaning, purpose and options. And your destiny is in your hands. Alex Cameron sums it up well: "You've got to find your place in the world. People are going to put you in a place until you decide what place you want to have."

The journey to purpose is our life's quest. It is the hero's journey. Game Changer John Mackey said, "We are all on a hero's journey. We just don't know it. Some answer the call, and some don't." Will you answer the call? In the final moments of your life, remembering your journey, will you smile with the knowledge that you chose to follow your dreams, to give your best and highest contribution, and to live your greatness?

When I left home at age sixteen to embark on the journey of my life, I saw my father cry for the first time. He said to me, "My child, my hope for you is to always see the world with a sense of wonder, and my dream for you is to create magic wherever you shine your focus." Today, as you embark on your journey to greatness, I send you off with the same sentiment. My hope for you is to always see the world with a sense of wonder. My dream for you is to create magic wherever you shine your focus.

THE GAME CHANGER'S PLEDGE

I am a Game Changer.

I choose to live by design, not default.

I am an original expression of humanity.

I have something significant to contribute to my family,
my community and my world.

I joyfully and audaciously pursue my passion.

I may tire and rest, but I never give up.

I stand tall on the shoulders of Game Changers before me.

I pay it forward by helping other Game Changers recognize
and embrace their true worth.

I place the best interests of our planet above
all considerations.

I use my gifts with humility and gratitude.

I am a Game Changer.

I am here to make a difference!

ACKNOWLEDGMENTS

I would like to thank the many founding members of my tribe, the many champions, believers, mentors, teachers and friends who made my vision possible. Without all of you, this book wouldn't have happened. The list is too long to include, but I'll do my best. I am most grateful to my mother, whose classroom I was in well before I ever caught the entrepreneurial bug.

My thanks to Mrs. Marie Agyeman, one of my first role models at Holy Child Secondary School, for demonstrating with class how to be an intelligent lady, and to Justice Brobbey, for helping me get back to the United States. I had the rare opportunity to watch *Coming to America* at your home, filling me with inspiration on my journey.

Thanks to the Codys, for making my American Dream a reality by inviting me to stay with you in South Carolina. Without your assurance and generosity there is no way my parents would have allowed me to journey to the United States. I am especially grateful to Sarah Cody, for being a friend and sister to me. Thanks too to the Cooper and Gibson families, who became my second family in South Carolina.

My thanks to Laurie Clark, Leslie Hielema, Sandra Peart, Kim Johnson, Sherman Wright, Courtney Counts and Alexandra Cameron, for being mentors, teachers and champions.

Thanks to Dondria Wallace, for teaching me how to be a leader, airman and strong woman of elegance.

I thank Juli Baldwin, my coach in writing this book. Thank you for pulling out of me what I didn't know existed, and helping bring order and discipline to the writing process, Thanks for your advice, insight and expertise in making this project fun and exciting. I have truly come to see you as a dear friend and greatly respect and admire your wonderful and unique gift.

I thank Inga McMichael and all the wonderful people I worked with at the U.S. Department of State as a speaker on behalf of our great country. Without the thousands of people from the many countries who entrusted me with their pain, questions, hopes and dreams, I wouldn't have considered writing this book.

I am grateful to Lori Hunter, whom I met at Syracuse University as the dean of electrical engineering. Thank you for your unwavering support and guidance, and for becoming a big sister to me.

Thanks to Dr. Shihab Ghaya, for always welcoming me to your office hours with a big smile, taking the time to teach me the fundamentals of electromagnetics, and making me a priority.

My thanks to David Muir, for being a friend and sharing with me the nuggets of knowledge you found along the way. I learned a lot from you; our friendly competition propelled me to do better than I envisioned myself capable of, and led me to recognize the vast potential of the Internet.

My thanks to the crew at Mini Circuits Labs, for my first taste of electronics, and especially to George Grant, for being a good friend.

My thanks to Charles Biney, Kelly Piegsa, Mekita Davis, Cory Turner, Wanto Wijea, Chulaphan Clark and R Maina, for your support at various points in my life.

Thanks to Dean Rychlik, for being the first to suggest that I was meant for something more. Wayne Tucker, you've known me longer than anyone else and have always been my biggest supporter and true friend, always maintaining that I would shine no matter what.

My heartfelt thanks goes to my buddies Cheryl Berry, Jamilia Walcot, Krishna O'Neal, Shenetta Gorden, Suzie Vigon and Jacquelyn White, for your friendship, unwavering faith, commitment and loyalty over the years. I love you all. Thanks to Yvette Thomas, for being a sister all these years, and to Paul Nicolini, for being in the trenches through the good and the bad.

My thanks to Paula White. The year we lived together was an accelerated life boot camp. You are one of the wisest and most intriguing people I know.

My thanks to Dr. Paul G. Steffes, for allowing me to work in your lab on the Search for Extraterrestrial Intelligence (SETI) project at Georgia Tech, where my love for deep space science grew exponentially. Your acumen, knowledge and curiosity compelled me to want to do more and be more.

My thanks to Suzy (Allen) Spang and Gloria Lequang, for welcoming me into your wonderful city and for truly championing my vision. You have made a tremendous impact on my company and on me. I am most grateful.

My thanks to JP and Barrett, for giving me the opportunity to get back in the game. JP, your spirit of lifelong learning, your insight and your amazing sense of humor impress me. A special thanks to Francesca, for putting up with all the time required by our work.

I am truly grateful to my family; my nieces and nephews, for making me proud each day, keeping me young and willing me to be a mentor for all of you. Special thanks to Lydia Ofori-Spio, for all your help, including transcribing my many interviews, and to Kyon, for keeping me on top of cool video games.

Thank you to my good friend and the most brilliant writer I know, Christina Edwards, for helping me birth Carmine St. Clair. I couldn't and wouldn't have completed *A Song for Carmine* without you.

I thank my parents for filling our home with joy, laughter and vision, and for housing and protecting our dreams, and helping us achieve them at great sacrifice.

The first book I ever read was a Penguin book. I remember the orange background and the iconic penguin imprinted on the back of it. I was too young then to remember today what the title was, but it was one of many books that my father had in his library. To be published by that same iconic imprint today is truly coming full circle and is a true honor, and I have Marian Lizzi and John Duff to thank for recognizing my message and helping me focus and create this book. I am especially grateful to Marian for your faith and belief in this project and your patience and enthusiasm that inspired me during this exciting new chapter in my life.

NOTES

INTRODUCTION

"Half of New Graduates Are Jobless or Underemployed." *USA Today*. April 23, 2012. usatoday30.usatoday.com/news/nation/story/2012-04-22/college-grads-jobless/54473426/1.

Adams, Susan. "New Survey: Majority of Employees Dissatisfied." *Forbes*. May 18, 2012. forbes.com/sites/susanadams/2012/05/18/new-survey-majority-of-employees-dissatisfied.

UNBRIDLED CREATIVITY

Center for Human Imagination: imagination.ucsd.edu/about.html.

Text of Steve Jobs's Commencement Address (2005). *Stanford Report*. June 14, 2005. news.stanford.edu/news/2005/june15/jobs-061505.html.

Sabre, "Our History." sabre.com/index.php/about/our-history.

Graphene: World-Leading Research and Development (University of Manchester): graphene.manchester.ac.uk.

RADICAL PASSION

Parker Brothers Concepts: parkerbrotherschopper.com.

Michael Jordan Biography: biography.com/people/michael-jordan-9358066.

Lake, Thomas. "Did This Man Really Cut Michael Jordan?" *Sports Illustrated*. January 16, 2012. si.com/vault/2012/01/16/106149626/did-this-man-really-cut-michael-jordan.

Urban Farmers: urbanfarmers.org.

The Dream Talks: thedreamtalks.com.

"Biography." Nelson Mandela Foundation. nelsonmandela.org/content/page/biography.

ACTIVE COMPASSION

Patricia Bath Biography: biography.com/people/patricia-bath-21038525.

Kiva: Loans That Change Lives: kiva.org.

Jackley, Jessica. "Poverty, Money—and Love." July 2010. ted.com/talks/jessica_
   jackley_poverty_money_and_love.

"Kiva and ProFounder—with Jessica Jackley." Mixergy. May 9, 2011. mixergy.
   com/jessica-jackley-kiva-interview.

Flannery, Matt. "Kiva and the Birth of Person-to-Person Microfinance."
   Innovations: Technology, Governance, Globalization 2, no. 1–2 (Winter 2007):
   31–56. doi:10.1162/itgg.2007.2.1-2.31.

Ekiel, Erika B. "Jessica Jackley: Stories of Poverty and Entrepreneurship." *Insights*
   by Stanford Business. May 7, 2013. gsb.stanford.edu/insights/jessica-jackley
   -stories-poverty-entrepreneurship.

Ramli, David. "How a Lonely Aussie Student Inspired $US19 Billion Whats
   App." Australian Breaking News Headlines & World News Online. February
   25, 2014. smh.com.au/business/how-a-lonely-aussie-student-inspired-us19
   -billion-whatsapp-20140225-33dst.html.

Olson, Parmy. "The Rags-to-Riches Tale of How Jan Koum Built WhatsApp into
   Facebook's New $19 Billion Baby." *Forbes*. February 19, 2014. forbes.com/
   sites/parmyolson/2014/02/19/exclusive-inside-story-how-jan-koum-built
   -whatsapp-into-facebooks-new-19-billion-baby.

Platt, Larry. "Magic Johnson Builds an Empire." *New York Times Magazine*.
   December 10, 2000. partners.nytimes.com/library/magazine/home/
   20001210mag-magicjohnson.html.

OBSESSIVE FOCUS

Tencent, "About Tencent." www.tencent.com/en-us/at/abouttencent.shtml.

Gallo, Carmine. "Steve Jobs: Get Rid of the Crappy Stuff." *Forbes*. May 16, 2011.
   forbes.com/sites/carminegallo/2011/05/16/steve-jobs-get-rid-of-the-crappy
   -stuff.

Wasserman, Todd. "WhatsApp Founders Are Low Key—And Now Very Rich."
   Mashable. February 19, 2014. mashable.com/2014/02/19/whatsapp-founders
   -jan-koum-brian-acton.

Houston, Drew. "Dropbox CEO Drew Houston's 2013 MIT Commencement
   Address Transcript." *Network World*. June 7, 2013. networkworld.com/

article/2167075/infrastructure-management/dropbox-ceo-drew-houston-s
-2013-mit-commencement-address-transcript.html.

RELENTLESS HUSTLE

Schoenberger, Chana R. "Out of Context." *Forbes*. November 29, 2004. forbes
.com/forbes/2004/1129/064.html.

"Kenny Chesney Is Billboard Artist of the Millennium Thanks to 'Somewhere
with You.'" *Taste of Country*. February 9, 2011. tasteofcountry.com/kenny
-chesneys-billboard-artist-of-the-millennim.

Crandell, Ben. "The Kenny Chesney Reboot." SouthFlorida.com. April 11, 2013.
southflorida.com/events/go-guide-blog/sf-tortuga-music-festival-kenny
-chesney-interview-20130411,0,3085499.story.

"All Access on Walmart Soundcheck: Kenny Chesney on Playing Concerts Both
Big and Small." July 16, 2012. youtube.com/watch?v=0H1mAU47bg0.

Geron, Tomio. "Mark Zuckerberg: Don't Just Start a Company, Do Something
Fundamental." *Forbes*. October 20, 2012. forbes.com/sites/tomiogeron/
2012/10/20/mark-zuckerberg-dont-just-start-a-company-do-something
-fundamental.

Mark Zuckerberg Biography: biography.com/people/mark-zuckerberg-507402.

Lagorio-Chafkin, Christine. "How Shutterstock Went from Zero to IPO." *Inc*.
October 29, 2012. inc.com/christine-lagorio/bootstrappers-bible-shutter
stock-founder-success-story.html.

Durgy, Edwin. "Oh Snap! Shutterstock Founder Jon Oringer Is a Billionaire."
Forbes. June 28, 2013. forbes.com/sites/edwindurgy/2013/06/28/oh-snap
-shutterstock-founder-jon-oringer-is-a-billionaire.

EXTREME AUDACITY

Patricia Bath Biography: biography.com/people/patricia-bath-21038525.

Johnston, David Cay. "Rene Anselmo, 69, the Founder of a Satellite Network, Is
Dead." *New York Times*. September 20, 1995. nytimes.com/1995/09/21/
obituaries/rene-anselmo-69-the-founder-of-a-satellite-network-is-dead.html.

"PanAmSat Shifts to Cautious Growth from Bold Innovation." *Satellite*.
September 27, 2004. satellitetoday.com/publications/st/feature/2004/09/27/
panamsat-shifts-to-cautious-growth-from-bold-innovation.

Scullard, Howard Hayes. "Scipio Africanus the Elder." Encyclopedia Britannica

Online. May 13, 2013. britannica.com/EBchecked/topic/529046/Scipio
-Africanus-the-Elder.

McCracken, Harry, and Lev Grossman. "Google vs. Death." *Time*. September 30,
2013. time.com/574/google-vs-death.

Levy, Steven. "Google's Larry Page on Why Moon Shots Matter." *Wired*. January
15, 0013. wired.com/2013/01/ff-qa-larry-page.

BeLoved, "Our Founder's Story." belovedxxx.com/business/about/sandra.

Danica Patrick Biography: biography.com/people/danica-patrick-201312.

PIT BULL TENACITY

Wright, Eric. "Waymon Armstrong Engineers New Virtual Reality." *I4 Business*.
September 30, 2013. i4biz.com/people_companies/waymon-armstrong
-engineers-new-virtual-reality.

DISCOVER YOUR GREATNESS

Searching for Sugar Man: sonyclassics.com/searchingforsugarman/site/.

"Alexandra Cameron." Businessweek.com. investing.businessweek.com/research/
stocks/people/person.asp?personId=50911585&ticker=EMMS&previousCap
Id=28028&previousTitle=Emmis%20Communications%20Corp.

Loud Digital: louddigital.tv.

EMBRACE YOUR DIFFERENCE

White, James. "The Story Behind Rocky." *Total Film*. October 26, 2009. totalfilm
.com/features/the-story-behind-rocky.

Yummly, "About Yummly." info.yummly.com/about.

LIVE YOUR LIFE BY DESIGN

Ben Silbermann Keynote Address at Alt Summit: vimeo.com/user10165343/
review/35759983/820bd84fa4.

Lagorio-Chafkin, Christine. "How Fear of Embarrassment Kept Pinterest Alive."
Inc. March 15, 2012. inc.com/christine-lagorio/pinterest-ben-silbermann
-talks-building-his-company.html.

Miller, Michael J. "Intel Enters Smartphone Chip Race for Real." PCMag.com.
January 11, 2012. forwardthinking.pcmag.com/ces/292745-intel-enters
-smartphone-chip-race-for-real.

"Infographic: 2013 Mobile Growth Statistics." Digital Buzz Blog. October 1, 2013. digitalbuzzblog.com/infographic-2013-mobile-growth-statistics.

"Birth of the Internet." PBS. pbs.org/transistor/background1/events/arpanet.html.

Knoblauch, Max. "A Brief History of the Domain Name." Mashable. March 10, 2014. mashable.com/2014/03/10/domain-names-history.

"The Size of the World Wide Web (The Internet)." June 5, 2014. worldwideweb size.com.

Envato: envato.com/about.

Simpson, David. "Donors Smash Goal for School Hero Antoinette Tuff's Fund for Inner-city Kids." CNN. August 29, 2013. cnn.com/2013/08/28/justice/georgia-school-shooting-hero. *The link to donate is gofundme.com/41fqvw#.*

Kaufman, Micha. "The Vision Behind the New Fiverr." Official Fiverr Blog. June 25, 2013. blog.fiverr.com/the-vision-behind-the-new-fiverr.

DeAmicis, Carmel. "Once Upon a Time the Founder of Freelancing Site Fiverr Was a Lawyer." PandoDaily. August 12, 2013. pando.com/2013/08/12/once-upon-a-time-the-founder-of-freelancing-site-fiverr-was-a-lawyer.

FIND YOUR TRIBE

SCORE: score.org.

Beier, Chris, and Daniel Wolfman. "What Happened When Grooveshark Couldn't Meet Payroll." *Inc.* May 24, 2012. inc.com/chris-beier-and-dan-wolfman/grooveshark-sam-tarantino-what-happened-when-couldnt-meet-payroll.html.

Beier, Chris, and Daniel Wolfman. "The Unexpected Meeting with Esther Dyson That Saved Flickr." *Inc.* May 24, 2012. inc.com/chris-beier-and-daniel-wolfman/caterina-fake-flickr-esther-dyson-pc-forum.html.

Olson, Parmy. "The Rags-to-Riches Tale of How Jan Koum Built WhatsApp into Facebook's New $19 Billion Baby." *Forbes.* February 19, 2014. forbes.com/sites/parmyolson/2014/02/19/exclusive-inside-story-how-jan-koum-built-whatsapp-into-facebooks-new-19-billion-baby.

Smith, David. "Proof! Just Six Degrees of Separation Between Us." *Guardian.* August 3, 2008. theguardian.com/technology/2008/aug/03/internet.email.

Bosker, Bianca. "Facebook Shrinks 'Six Degrees of Separation' to Just 4.74." *Huff-*

ington Post. November 22, 2011. huffingtonpost.com/2011/11/22/facebook
-six-degrees-separation_n_1107577.html.

Beier, Chris, and Daniel Wolfman. "This Guy Invented the iPod with Steve Jobs."
Inc. May 31, 2012. inc.com/chris-beier-and-daniel-wolfman/apple-ipod
-inventor-tony-fadell-innovation.html.

START WHERE YOU ARE

Welch, Liz. "How I Did It: Eileen Fisher." *Inc.* November 1, 2010. inc.com/
magazine/20101101/how-i-did-it-eileen-fisher.html.

"Pierre Omidyar Interview." Academy of Achievement. October 27, 2000.
achievement.org/autodoc/printmember/omi0int-1.

Beier, Chris. "Eileen Fisher: 'Thinking About Death Made Me Think About
What Really Mattered.'" *Inc.* March 24, 2014. inc.com/chris-beier/eileen
-fisher-fashion-entrepreneur-employee-stock-ownership-plan.html.

Okura, Lynn. "Eckhart Tolle on the Small Steps That Lead to Greatness (Video)."
Huffington Post. May 16, 2014. huffingtonpost.com/2014/05/16/eckhart
-tolle-a-new-earth_n_5339783.html.

Ekiel, Erika B. "Jessica Jackley: Stories of Poverty and Entrepreneurship." *Insights*
by Stanford Business. May 7, 2013. gsb.stanford.edu/insights/jessica-jackley
-stories-poverty-entrepreneurship.

"TIME Talks to Google CEO Larry Page About Its New Venture to Extend Human Life." *Time*. September 18, 2013. business.time.com/2013/09/18/google
-extend-human-life/.

Whole Foods Market History: wholefoodsmarket.com/company-info/whole
-foods-market-history.

INDEX

Page numbers in *italics* indicate figures.

Flannery, Matthew, 54
Fleming, Alexander, 3
flesh, audacity in the, 97–100
Flickr, 187, 188
Florida, 175
Florida Digital Network, 85–86, 114
focusing on where you're going, 64–66
    See also obsessive focus
Foot Locker, 138–39
Ford, Henry, 3
Forrest Gump (movie), 70
founders of the tribe, 185–88
14 Business, 116
freelance websites, 85, 171, 175, 211
free streaming music, 184
fund-raising websites, 176

Gagarin, Yuri, 5
Galai, Yaron, 77–78
Gallagher, Mike, 22, 44, 83–86, 108–9,
    114, 131
"game," 9
Game Changers, x–xii, 1–10
    "category of one," 46, 125
    entrepreneurs, ix, xi, 2, 8, 32–33, 80–81,
        122, 135, 215
    evolving the system by, 33–34
    innovation, x, 2, 8, 15, 29, 83, 149–50,
        157
    journey, 104–5, 143–46, 209–14
    Pledge, 221
    potential, discovering your greatness,
        129, 129, 132–34, 140, 141, 141,
        142–43, 145–46, 169, 180
    problem solvers, 56, 80–84, 85, 135–37
    uncommon success achieved by, xi, 2,
        3–4, 6–8, 9, 10
    you are a changer, 9–10
    See also action; breaking through to
        uncommon success; passion; purpose;
        7 key traits that fuel Game Changers'
        success; Spio, Mary A.
Gandhi, Mahatma, 3, 9, 137
Gates, Bill, 2, 3, 9, 21–22, 23, 26, 27, 71,
    78, 92, 107, 193
Gaza, 55, 78
Geim, Andre, 28

Gen2Media (Vidaroo), 8, 106–7, 119–21,
    143, 195
Georgia Tech, 7
geosynchronous orbit (Clarke Orbit), 16,
    17
getting audacious, 100–101
Ghana, West Africa, x, 2, 4, 5, 16, 45, 47,
    48, 55, 158, 159, 177, 178, 193, 213
glaucoma, 52
global freelancing, 176–77
global satellite system (privately owned), 94
goal, obsessive focus, 64–66
Golden Globe Awards, 145
Google, 17, 65, 69, 88, 95–97, 135, 138,
    149, 168, 169, 183, 203, 215
Graj, Noah, 38–40, 56, 91, 92–93, 111,
    142, 151, 218
Graj + Gustavsen, 38, 142
Grammy Awards, 145
graphene, 28–29
greatest point of contribution, discovering
    your greatness, 129, 129, 130, 140–
    43, 141, 170
greatness, 128–30, 129
    See also discovering your greatness
Grooveshark, 184–85, 188
growth, passion for, 38–40

Hannibal, 57, 95
happiness, x, 49
Harlem, New York, 61
harnessing your inner pit bull, 116–18
Harris Corp., 171
Harvard, 70–71, 77, 78, 92, 174, 209
HBO, 7
help (asking for) finding your tribe, 181–85
Hemingway, Ernest, 16
heroes (amplifiers), finding your tribe,
    xi–xii, 191, 192–94
Heroku, 183
Hielema, Leslie, 122
Himalayas, 175
hip-hop music, 110, 144–45
Hispanic cultural trends, 34
historical Game Changers, 3
HMV, 61
Hoffman, Reid, 199

ABOUT THE AUTHOR

Mary Spio was born in Syracuse, New York, to Ghanaian parents. Growing up in Ghana, Mary didn't see her first computer until she was seventeen, yet she became a deep space engineer, designing and launching communication satellites. At Boeing, she helped pioneer digital technology that redefined how major motion pictures are distributed to movie theaters throughout the world. From there, she focused on her passion for matchmaking and founded One2One.com, a specialty media company dedicated to resources for singles. Mary also founded Gen2Media (now Vidaroo), an emerging leader in the digital media industry. Leveraging the power of online video, search and social media, Mary's companies provide engaging user experiences for consumers and deliver quantifiable results for some of the most iconic brands, high-profile entertainers and events in the world, including Microsoft Xbox, Walmart, Toyota, Coca-Cola, Justin Timberlake, Will Smith, Britney Spears and the Billboard Awards show. She is currently CEO of Next Galaxy, a virtual reality company.